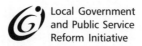

Local Government
and Public Service
Reform Initiative

CW00693736

Navigation to the Market

Regulation and Competition
in Local Utilities
in Central and Eastern Europe

Edited by

GÁBOR PÉTERI–TAMÁS M. HORVÁTH

Second edition

LOCAL GOVERNMENT AND PUBLIC SERVICE REFORM INITIATIVE
OPEN SOCIETY INSTITUTE

Address
Nádor utca 11.
H-1051 Budapest, Hungary

Mailing address
P.O. Box 519
H-1357 Budapest, Hungary

Telephone
(36-1) 327-3104

Fax
(36-1) 327-3105

E-mail
lgprog@osi.hu

Web Site
http://lgi.osi.hu

Second Edition—CD attached

First published in 2001
by Local Government and Public Service Reform Initiative, Open Society Institute–Budapest

© OSI/LGI, 2001

OPEN SOCIETY INSTITUTE

The publication of these country reports has been funded by the British Department for International Development and the Local Government and Public Service Reform Initiative of the Open Society Institute in Budapest within the framework of the Local Government Policy Partnership Programme. The judgements expressed herein do not necessarily reflect the views of the above two sponsors.

Copies of the book can be ordered by e-mail or post from LGI.
Printed in Budapest, Hungary, March 2003.
Design & Layout by Createch Ltd.

Contents

List of Tables and Figures

TABLES

CHAPTER 5

CHAPTER 6

CHAPTER 7

CHAPTER 8

FIGURES

Foreword

This book was prepared under the "Local Government Policy Partnership" Program, which is a joint project of two donor organizations. The British Government's Department for International Development (DFID), and the Local Government and Public Service Initiative (LGI) of the Open Society Institute, Budapest launched this regional program. The "Local Government Policy Partnership" (LGPP) projects intend to contribute to policy development and innovation in these countries.

LGPP hopes to develop expertise and to support professional cooperation among local government specialists throughout Central and Eastern Europe. Parallel to this, experiences from this region should be made available in Central and Eastern Europe, and in Central Asia. The core partner countries are the Czech Republic, Hungary, Poland and Slovakia. However, other countries have been invited to participate in these regional projects, which would help direct information exchange and comparison of policy efforts. Planned LGPP publications include policy studies and proposals discussed with government officials and experts in the countries involved.

Targeted beneficiaries of LGPP projects are national government ministries, local government associations, research and training institutions, and individual local authorities throughout the CEE region. LGPP intends to publish studies every three years. In 2001-2002, (the first year of LGPP operations), the following policy areas were selected:

a)   Education financing and management;

b)   Regulation and competition of local utility services, and

c)   Public perception of local governments.

Readers of this publication will find detailed information on utility and communal services from the Czech Republic, Hungary, Latvia, Poland, Romania and Slovakia. As access to information is critical for transparent management of these urban services, a separate chapter is devoted to this topic. In the introductory part the two managers of the project have formulated several policy recommendations on various aspects of regulation and competition rules in the local public utility and communal sectors.

Ken Davey & Gábor Péteri

November, 2001

11

Regulation and Competition in the Local Utility Sector in Central and Eastern Europe

Tamás M. Horváth, Gábor Péteri

Table of Contents

Regulation and Competition in the Local Utility Sector in Central and Eastern Europe

Tamás M. Horváth, Gábor Péteri

1. INTRODUCTION

Local public utility and communal services are the focus of this report. They are regarded as basic services in the studied six countries of Central and Eastern Europe (CEE). Water services, regular solid waste collection and disposal, district heating, public cleaning, management of social housing, public transportation, and so on, are all a part of the everyday lives of ordinary citizens. However, there are great differences in the manner in which these services are provided, and there is still much confusion in approaches, objectives and policies as to how these activities should be managed and financed.

In this publication, we deal with local public utilities and communal services, which are specific branches of the utility sector. During the changes of the past decade, public utilities have also been under transformation worldwide. The public utility sector still has its own problems in this period of rapid technological change with the increasing dependence of the economy on energy, along with the development of global networks. The role of the private sector has to be identified within the framework of public functions of the welfare state.

The future of urban services (local public utilities, communal services) in the CEE countries raise even more specific problems than the transformation of the utility sector. These changes are implemented in a decentralized political and administrative environment, which further complicates existing problems. Economic and management decisions are always influenced by local politics, which does not help the economically rational design of service provision.

Political considerations and traditions led to fragmented and—from an economic point of view—small size service providers. Political goals of accountability and public control of local governments are in conflict with the economies of scale arguments. New political and administrative mechanisms have to be developed, in order to achieve efficient service provision.

Conditions of local decision-making further complicates the transformation of these services. At local governments the roles of owner, budget designer and social service provider are mixed. These three functions have to be balanced in each local decision. Operational rules of municipalities are influenced by other factors, for example the specific conditions for managing conflicts of interest, lack of professional capacity, and so on.

However, it is precisely these nuances and complexities of this topic that makes it all the more challenging and interesting. We hope that the target audience of this book will be broad. This information on Central Eastern European countries might be useful for policy analysts, who are interested in various aspects of local public utility services. Discussion of the linkages between various regulatory mechanisms and on service management issues will help the policy makers as well. Regulatory policies and specific rules of service delivery are rather diverse in the CEE region, so this book will support the information exchange amongst experts. Beside national government officials it will also be informative for local practitioners.

The subject of the research is the role of public influence in the transformation of local infrastructure. It is a topic with many conflicts, because as state functions decrease, they need to be replaced by private actions and new types of policymaking should be developed. Our approach in this study is that changes in the utility and communal sectors are prerequisites of transformation in the public sector as a whole. For improving public utilities, consequent and persistent government policy is needed. The specific objectives of these studies are:

i)   to make an inventory on the present status of local public utility service management;

ii)   to identify those areas of local public utilities which are required to develop efficient and high quality service provision in the emerging market environment, in the current stage of decentralization. This critical assessment leads to stage (iii);

iii)   policy proposals, which will lead to the real transformation of this sector.

Despite the present strong incentives and pressure, conditions have not, as yet, been guaranteed in the researched countries. There are many controversial circumstances preventing development from turning into the direction of modern welfare economies. Drawbacks are different by sectors and by countries.

We are aware of the fact, that a description of these local utility and communal services will not lead to general conclusions on all the studied sectors. Special characteristics of these activities do not allow a comprehensive analysis. That is why we often make a reference to special features of technology or to specific country. But, we believe that we were able to identify a more or less complete list of issues in local public utility service provision.

During the past decade, the emphasis in public debate on utility services has been slightly modified in the CEE countries. At the first stage, and after the political changes, the primary goal was to improve the service efficiency; to utilize the benefits of the decentralized system and private institutions for achieving a better performance of services.

There is no comprehensive and reliable information on the efficiency gains of the transformation of public utility and communal services in the CEE countries. So we cannot evaluate the impact of these changes, but evidence from other countries, which have already been through this transformation, show a significant reduction of costs. For example, an OECD study on solid waste management has proved that a private collection of communal waste results in 15–40% percent lower costs than a public collection.[1]

Despite these facts, the political and public debate on local public utilities has been slightly modified during the past few years. Without having specific information on efficiency gains and improvement of service performance, equity and affordability came into the focus point of discussions. These arguments do not seem to appreciate the impact of privatization on the level of public utility services, but they raise different issues.

This second stage of service transformation (regulation, competition, contracting) was the focus of our research. We believe that advantages of the private sector can be realized in a properly designed public service environment. We do not want simply to neglect or to support private provision of utility services, but our goal is to discuss those components of regulation, which would protect the public interest, but do not destroy the market. This approach will hopefully support the public debate on these issues.

This fits into the theory of public sector management, focusing on communal and utility services. Management of economic and political transition in CEE countries gives the framework for the topics to be examined in this book. This particular viewpoint can be generalized, and it will be useful for a better understanding of more complex problems of the whole region in its transformation period.

Our aim is to draw conclusions on the relationship between the public and private sector by investigating specific issues in this area. This method will be more relevant than following some recent comments on the ranking of countries, or describing the present process as a race for joining various frameworks of international integration. However, in addition to the analyses, a normative character is also preferred in this study. We focus mainly on policy formulation at both government levels. Nevertheless, the authors recognize the limitations, but the aim is that a professional debate will be launched.

This comparative paper is based on country reports from six Central and Eastern European countries: the Czech Republic, Hungary, Latvia, Poland, Romania and Slovakia. There are differences in the selected countries according to their model of development, involvement in the EU integration process, historical heritage, and so on. However their common feature is their strong motivation to reform and transform their systems. We think this sample represents more or less other countries of the former 'Eastern block', at least in its European region. he authors are united in the opinion that conflicting situations commonly arise from similar challenges or problems.

Authors from the six countries—following an agreed outline—produced detailed comprehensive reports on local public utility and communal services. The approach and style of each paper is different, because the available information, the form of existing institutions, and the present problems varied regionally. This summary chapter is primarily based on the information collected by the national teams, but it was supplemented with other facts, collected from personal interviews in these countries and from the available literature. It has been discussed at a regional workshop with the authors and other experts.

This summary chapter is heavily based on the information collected by the country teams, so we are very grateful for their excellent work. The editors have visited the studied countries, and with the assistance of the country teams were able to collect information from practitioners. We are also grateful to Eva Voszka for commenting the earlier version of this summary chapter. Meetings with national and local government officials, service company managers, representatives of professional associations helped a lot to understand the reality. Any possible misinterpretation of the collected information is our responsibility.

2.   THEORETICAL FRAMEWORK

In classical theory market failures arise from the production of public goods and other operating mechanisms of society. There are several limitations like natural monopolies, externalities and information asymmetry on the market[2]. There are different linkages among these phenomena, for instance, the production of public goods generally involves externalities[3] for example services which provide additional benefits for specific users, which then has an impact on income distribution, which is either accepted by the public bodies or has some favorable macroeconomic effects (on unemployment, inflation, et cetera).

What is the basic characteristic feature of public utility and communal services from the point of view of market failures? Most of them are public goods, because government actions are needed in the production and distribution; natural monopolies dominate the network based services; and to a lesser extent externalities and information asymmetry exists.

According to public sector economics[4] social or public-good consumption benefits are available in a non-competitive manner. Market failure occurs in the provision of public goods, because individual consumers will act as free riders. For efficient provision of public goods, a political process of allocation is needed.

"A public good is a good or service that provides benefits which cannot be limited to those who directly pay for it".[5] The government is involved in the production of public goods. In a pure case consumption is realized collectively by all people, notwithstanding payments.[6] Two basic characteristics of pure public goods are specified, such as non-excludability in consumption and joint use of goods and services. According to the well-known typology[7] apart from specific public and private goods, common pool and toll goods are also distinguished.

'Pure' public goods are relatively rare, typically public characteristics are mixed with private features. These mixed goods are characterized by different scale of joint consumption. Only in extreme cases is individual consumption excluded absolutely, so the level of excludability makes the real difference between public and private services.

According to Savas (1987) the separation of service provision and production is a further dimension, differentiating public and private functions. From this aspect linkages to the public bodies are crucial and they are more important than ideal-typical forms of private and public goods. This concept argues that public provision does not mean necessarily governmental production of goods and services. Governments are more service managers, facilitators using the private sector for producing public services[8]

The other most relevant market failure in natural monopoly services is the neglected competition. Natural monopolistic character of public utilities is a more significant feature of these services, than the scale of government involvement in production of services and goods. According to Stiglitz, we talk about natural monopoly, "when a firm has attained its monopoly position as a result of increasing returns to scale".[9]

In all cases of market failures, government actions are needed. The content and focus of public activities depend on the nature of market failures. Natural monopolies and public (or mixed) goods and services in urban areas more precisely consist of the following:

i)   Urban public utility services as natural monopolies:
*   healthy drinking water supply;
*   sewage;
*   district heating;
*   electricity;
*   urban gas supply.

ii)   Urban public utility services as specifically public goods:
*   public lighting;
*   rain-water drainage;
*   public cleaning;
*   urban (non-toll) roads.

iii)   Urban communal services as mixed (not-specifically public) goods:

- public park and green;

- public cemeteries;

- solid waste removal and disposal;

- individual liquid waste removal and disposal;

- (social) housing maintenance;

- public chimney cleaning and supervision of heating facilities;

- public transport.

It should be noted in point i), that in urban areas a healthy drinking water supply, sewage, rainwater drainage and district heating are typically provided as natural monopolies under local or regional management. Electricity and urban gas are slightly different, because the provision of these services are supplied mainly at the national level, and less by municipalities and other regional governments.

The characteristics and scale of public services and especially natural monopolies are changing. The recent trends in regulatory systems and ownership structures have developed a new environment for classical natural monopolies. Large networks are owned and operated by big national or international companies. In parallel to these changes, regulations force third party access to networks, which might limit the monopolistic character of the network based service provision.

Public functions are very different in each sector mentioned above. For instance, electricity has not been fully privately owned. Gas utilities have been privatized in some of the studied countries. In their case, the regulatory functions have been changed intensively. Models of public involvement do not depend only on sectors, but they are also influenced by historical development. Former publicly owned utilities can be transferred to the private sector quickly in the privatization process, but government regulatory functions are changing slowly.

The public character of services depends on three basic conditions. First of all ownership matters, but also the style and form of regulations have a strong impact on service provision. Secondly, private or public character of service production is very much influenced by several elements of the regulatory system: licensing, access to networks, price setting authority etc.). Finally, the method of financing greatly matters (i.e. whether services are financed through national and local taxes or user charges).

As these factors can be changed during the transformation of service provision, the characteristics of goods provided by natural monopolies changes gradually. As far as basic feature of goods provided by utility networks is concerned, the borderline between public and private is also modifiable. In the modernization process of natural monopolies, the main tendency is to split marketable, competitive activities from publicly owned and managed assets. For this purpose, exclusion from access to goods and services (networks) should be guaranteed. This general tendency is also expected in the provision of urban services. Under state socialism in its classical period, public services were mostly common pool goods. Consumption was not limited by the symbolic price. In the period of so called 'market socialism' some changes did begin, however, clear excludability has been implemented for the years of transition, after a reorganization of service provision. Changes can be illustrated with characteristics of goods and services provided by utility works (Figure 1.1).

Figure 1.1
Direction of the Change of Services Provided by Natural Monopolies in Transitive Economies

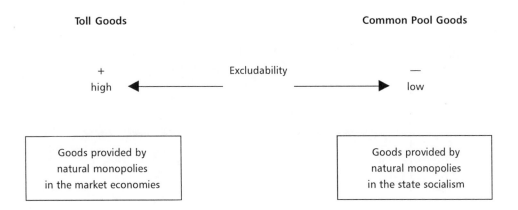

In point ii) above, it should be noted that in the case of specifically public goods, the market failure does not link to the position of natural monopolies. Specific public goods are relatively restricted at this level, because public goods can be provided by more aggregate (national or federal) level of government. Defence, police and prisons are typically managed by central government and administration. In relation to these type of services, it can be highlighted that public characters are more important in the practice than ideal-typical forms.

In point iii) above, it can be noted that as far as mixed goods are concerned, two main different factors may work against market failures. Firstly, the existence of the public client (the municipality) limits competition because of the missing cost saving interest. The second factor is the necessary joint provision, for ensuring the economies of scale rationale and restricting the competition (e.g. in waste collection, public transportation).

Local public goods and services are typically mixed. The extent and content of public provision is different by sectors. Additionally, the public character is changing historically. In a more developed stage of market economy in these countries, communal goods and services can be characterized according to Figure 1.2. The figure shows that stage, when some of the services have been privatized as a whole or partially. We used Savas's typology as a basis,[10] however it has to be changed according to the characteristics of service provision in the region.

Figure 1.2
The Nature of Communal Goods and Service

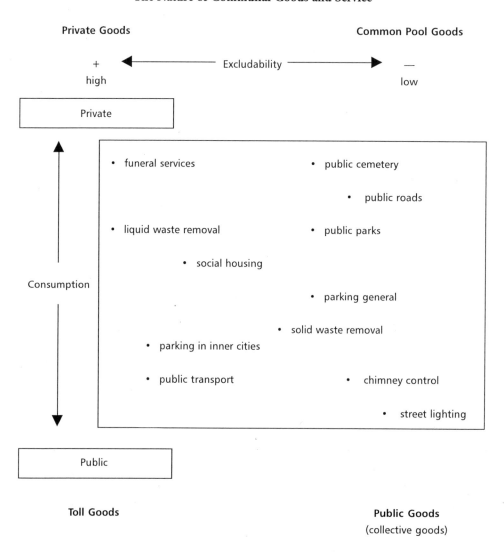

In a denationalized environment, in spite of possible privatization, particular government functions must remain such as pricing, involvement of the government in service development, consumer protection, et cetera, because under free market circumstances these tasks are not fulfilled. Roles of the general public are different by sectors, stage of development and country specifications. However, there is a common tendency, which is similar in developed Western economies and transforming countries, that has changed the character of mixed goods: that is the increasing role of exclusion and private consumption.

Motivation and social frameworks of these changes are very different. From a welfare state to the post-welfare, the development of economics is motivated by the intention to stop the overspending of the state budget. In transition economies, the main task is to transform the former centralized service assignment systems. From this respect, private roles in public provision could be more politicized, incentives for efficient services are less highlighted, partly because of the higher costs of reconstruction. In many respects, practitioners have to face similar challenges as does the modernization process of a few countries of the third world. Nevertheless, a common tendency of widely accepted direction to the expected development can be sketched. A lot of goods that used to be public goods or common pool goods become toll goods or private goods, such as social dwellings, public transport, clean water, et cetera. Formerly toll goods become 'pure' private goods in some cases, especially funeral services, health services of baths, et cetera. These tendencies are showed in Figure 1.3.

In public service provision, private characteristics and exclusion in consumption is becoming increasingly important. As we shall see from the country examples some of the urban public services have already been made private. It is implemented in two ways. One form is to decrease the amount of public or mixed goods, like the sale of the great part of social housing stock. The other is to eliminate particular services as public ones, for example cultural centers as institutions in transition countries, and to transfer all these services to the group of private services, which are supposed to be provided by the market.

The other form is the involvement of private service organizations in the service production, but keeping the public control over service performance, financing, quality control, et cetera. Privatization is not the only solution for cutting back on public spending. Another widely used policy is to prefer market based instruments in remaining a part of the public sector: creating incentives for competition; establishing independent regulatory functions; widening contractual relationships; and so on. These critical elements of private sector involvement are in the background of the changing character of services, when they move from public goods to toll goods.

Intervention may also lead to government failures. There are a few groups of theories focusing on this issue.[11] Although the main problems analyzed in our comparative project may fit properly into the theoretical framework described above, what so far has been less highlighted are the actual differences to be found in the social and economic systems.

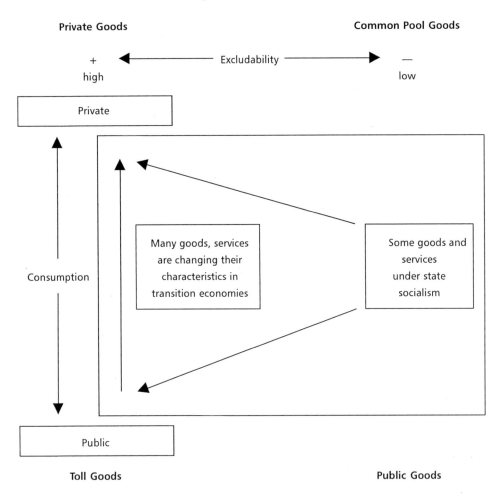

Figure 1.3
Change of Communal Goods

Both welfare state and socialism are criticized because of their exaggerated intervention. However, influencing the conditions of existing market systems is not the same task as replacing regulatory mechanisms in a command economy. Therefore—despite some similarities—the challenge to change the previous regimes is different to some extent.

Through destroying state-owned structures from the previous regime, governments find themselves with highly complicated reorganization tasks. In the case of CEE countries, the disintegration of the command economy is also linked to establishing market conditions and new public positions in public service provision at the same time. That is why West-European examples on market orientation in the public sector cannot be applied directly, because their reforms were built on a relatively plural structure of service provision. There was no need to restructure the basic social structure of property or institutional framework of public involvement. For the further analyses it is better to make a distinction between traditional government failures and 'state' failures, as that type of public failure which originated under state socialism. In the latter case, a correction of failures is directly linked to the wide restructuring of extremely nationalized ownership structures.

3. PROVISION OF URBAN SERVICES IN CEE COUNTRIES

What is the relevant framework of local service provision? According to Oates' (1972) decentralization theorem, each service should be provided in that area where costs and benefits have arisen in an optimal way. In the case of the transformation in CEE countries, this question is raised as the allocation of power and assignment of functions to different levels and types of local governments. In Central and Eastern European countries, reallocation of public functions was realized in a parallel way with division of functions.

A new allocation is based very much on the general level of development. Its known crucial character is the political, economic and social transformation process in the 1990s. The beginning of changes was a purely political process [Ágh, 1998]. It meant that crucial changes in social and economic circumstances were initiated by the political transformation, instead of a gradual development, by which 'revolutionary' institutional reforms could have been prepared.

Basic data are showed in Table 1.1–1.3 General characteristics of the studied countries as a sample of the whole region are as follows:

1. These are relatively underdeveloped countries in comparison to Western European ones. The urban population ratio is far from the developed level, as well as per capita GDP.

2. Transformation led to more serious decline because of the high social costs of restructuring. For example it is showed by unemployment rates. Some of the countries have already reached the pre-transition level of development and economic growth was begun. Others have not been out of the transformation shock, like Romania and Latvia.

3. The quality of urban infrastructure according to some basic parameters is also underdeveloped, although differences are higher to some extent, for example Czech indicators are closer to Western ones. At the other end of the scale, the Hungarian ratio of public sewerage services is unacceptably low. In these circumstances, it is difficult to make any general statement about the effectiveness of service delivery. Modernization should first focus on extending the delivery of some communal and utility services. Nevertheless, this task cannot be defined separately from the rationalization of the service provision.

Table 1.1
Selected Social Indicators, 1999 and 1990–1999

	Latvia	Poland	Slovakia	Hungary	Czech Republic	Romania
Population [in thousands]	2 389	38 741	5 381	10 075	10 263	22 402
Growth rate of population 1995–2000 [% per annum]	–1.5	0.1	0.1	–0.4	–0.2	–0.4
Life expectancy at birth [women and men, year]	74/62	77/68	77/69	75/67	77/70	74/66
Urban population [%]	69	64	57	63	75	55
Share of population in poverty [%]	23	13	1	2	1	30

SOURCES: World Statistics Pocketbook, 2000;
Nemzetközi Statisztikai Zsebkönyv, 1999;
Transition report, 2000, EBRD.

Table 1.2
Selected Economic Indicators, 1999

	Latvia	Poland	Slovakia	Hungary	Czech Republic	Romania
GDP/per capita [US$]	3 019	3 987	3 650	4 853	5 148	1 512
Level of real GDP (1989=100)	60	122	100	99	95	76
Unemployment [%]	14.0	10.4	15.6	7.8	7.5	10.4
Inflation [annual average consumer price level]	2.4	7.3	10.6	10.1	2.1	45.8
Cumulative foreign direct investment (1989–2000) per capita [US$]	1 027	751	669	1 935	2 102	303
Private sector share [%] in GDP (mid-2000)	65	70	75	80	80	60
Institutional performance of transition[12]	2.6	3.3	2.8	3.5	3.2	2.3

SOURCE: Transition report, 2000, EBRD.
Transition report update, 2001, EBRD.

Table 1.3

Selected Infrastructure Indicators, 1999 and 1990–1999

	Latvia	Poland	Slovakia[13]	Hungary	Czech Republic	Romania
Population [in thousands]	2,389	38 741	5 381	10 075	10 263	22 402
Dwellings supplied with water pipe network [%]	n. a.	89.8 C	82.3 G	84.6 E	96.9 A	51.4 B 54 F
Dwellings supplied with bath, shower [%]	n. a.	77.9 C	89.0 D	79.9 E	90.9 A	46.1 B
Dwellings supplied with WC [%]	n. a.	77.8 C	80.0 D	76.5 E	88.5 A	44.9 B
Dwellings supplied with central heating [%]	n. a.	68.4 C	74.7 D	48.2 E	59.0 A	38.9 B
Population connected to public sewerage network [%]	n. a.	46.6 D	54.7 G	22.0 E	59.2 E	51 F
Average of EBRD index of infrastructure reform	3.1	3.2	2.1	3.8	2.8	3.3
General government expenditures [% of GDP]	46.8	44.7	43.3	44.8	42.0	36.8

SOURCES: World Statistics Pocketbook, 2000.
　　　　　 Nemzetközi Statisztikai Zsebkönyv, 1999.
　　　　　 Transition report, 2000, EBRD.
　　　　　 Magyar Statisztikai Zsebkönyv, 1999.
　　　　　 Slovak data: Statistical Yearbook, 2000; Annual Bulletin EC, 1996.
　　　　　 A: 1991; B: 1992; C: 1995; D:1996; E: 1997; F: 2000; G: 1999.

This description of present and historically developed process shows that problems of the transition model are different from the Western one, because the circumstances and level of service provision are not the same. Liberalization of the market here serves first of all modernization, rather than improving the level of services. By modernization, we mean changes in methods of service provision, notwithstanding quality improvement. Above all, a particular environment of the market should be established. In the first stage, the existence of a sufficient number of providers was the question, because the market was absolutely virtual, it was monopolized by state-owned companies.

By the late 1990s, the number of providers increased in all these countries. Private service providers had a more active role. However, the remaining influence of state owned or regionally organized

29

public enterprises still exists, but it is different by countries. For instance, their role is more extended in Romania ('regie autonomes'), than in Slovakia or Poland. However, even in these latter ones there are sectors where privatization has not yet begun (for examples the provision of drinking water in Slovakia or electricity in both countries). Provision of public utility and communal services are divided amongst central and local governments, and, on the other hand, between different levels of local governments.

The typical feature of the CEE region is the crucial role of the basic (municipal) level of territorial governments [Horváth, 2000]. Most of the public utility and communal services are provided by municipal governments. Division of work is accepted only with state administration, and to a much lesser extent with higher territorial self-government level. The elected middle tier was typically weak in these countries in the first period of transformation.

This problem is important from the point of view of technical services, because the economies of scale is evidently linked to larger territories, i.e. to more integrated units of municipal governments, or to intermediary levels of government. The weakness of this form of integration leads paradoxically to better chances of integration, led by private service providers. The alternative option would have been service provision by the state administrative, which was not a preferred solution.

As far as the second main stage of local development is concerned, the re-establishment of middle tiers is highlighted. Based on the direction of recent changes it is hard to predict the future, modernization projects will probably be managed by new or newly strengthened levels of territorial governments. This progress of administrative regionalization is supported by the common aspirations of the European Union. Structural policies of the EU also focus on regional levels, as units of modernization.

Depending on the scale and form of decentralization, local governments play different roles in the financing and managing of local public utilities. The models of the six studied countries diverge by the forms of local service assignment; transfer of municipal property; and autonomy in local revenue raising. These indicators of decentralization are determined by general factors, like the share of local budgets in GDP and general government expenditures or the role of the intermediary level of government.

These two latter factors define the fiscal and legal environment for public utility services. After the first decade of transition the public sector has a similarly limited role in the economy. In most of these countries consolidated general government expenditures are 36%–44% of the gross domestic product. These figures show a substantial decrease in public expenditures, which used to dominate the economy through extensive redistribution under the communist systems. The reorganization of the state functions was implemented partly through decentralization and devolution. According to the scale of decentralization, the studied countries might be grouped into three categories. The share of local budget expenditures in relation to GDP are the highest in Hungary (12%) and Poland (12%). Two countries belong to the second group as well: Czech

Republic (7%) and Latvia (9%). The least decentralized countries are Romania and Slovakia, both of them with a 4% share of local expenditures in GDP.[14]

Another important factor of decentralization trends is the role and function of the intermediary level of government. The middle tier of the government had an important role in the service delivery and reallocation of resources under the Soviet rule. In the least decentralized countries, where the state administrative and local government functions are not clearly separated, the districts, counties, and regions dominantly have a non-elected administrative character. This is the case in both the Czech Republic and Slovakia, however, reforms are under completion.

Where the intermediary levels of sub-national government are elected and public functions are assigned to them, there the relationship between the municipal and county level matters. In Romania the 'judets' have broader functions and in Latvia the districts seem to have the inherited, informal functions of equalization, so they can influence the municipal decisions to a greater extent. In Hungary and Poland, the responsibilities and competencies of the middle level governments are clearly separated and no forms of subordination is accepted between the two levels of elected local government.

There is no detailed and comparable fiscal information on local utility services in the six studied countries. The terms and budget classification are diverse, so expenditures on local public utilities are found under different mixed categories, like communal services, municipal services, economic services, and so on. The available data shows that there are two groups of countries. In Hungary and Latvia local government budgets seem to play minor roles in utility services, as only 15–19% of local government expenditures are used for these services. In Poland and Slovakia the broadly interpreted municipal services are 29–44% of local government budgets. (see Table 1.4)

Table 1.4
Public Utility Expenditures in Local Budgets

HUNGARY			
FY 2000			Local government expenditures
Housing, community and public services:			6.6%
Economic functions:			10.9%
FY 1998	Current expenditures	Capital expenditures	Total expenditures
Housing	1.9%	5.1%	2.3%
Communal services	6.1%	10.7%	6.2%
Public transportation	1.2%	5.7%	1.9%
Water management	0.3%	21.4%	4.2%
Total	9.5%	42.9%	14.6%

Table 1.4 (continued)
Public Utility Expenditures in Local Budgets

LATVIA		
FY 1999		Self-government expenditures
Economic services		16%
Of which: housing, public utilities,		
environmental protection	93%	
Transportation, communication		3%
Total		19%

POLAND		
FY 1999		Local expenditures at gmina and powiat level
Municipal services		29%
		Capital expenditures
Gmina municipal services		16%
Poviat municipal services		14%

SLOVAKIA		
FY 1999		Local government expenditures
Local economic services		8.1%
Of which: Public lighting	3.5%	
Funeral services	0.6%	
Public welfare facilities	2.4%	
Environmental services		6.6%
Of which: Municipal solid waste management	2.5%	
Street cleaning and snow removal	2.1%	
Park maintenance	1.8%	
Water supply		2.1%
Housing construction and management		15.0%
Public transportation and road maintenance		12.2%
Total communal and utility services		44.0%

SOURCE: LGPP project country reports, 2001.

This data does not present the differences in local mandatory service competencies. In all the six countries, local governments have rather broad responsibilities in public service delivery, so not only these communal services, but also wide scale of human services (education, welfare and health services, etc) is decentralized (with some exceptions, like Slovakia, before the planned reform). A lower percentage of utility services in local budgets might reflect the differences in the organizational form of service delivery. A lower proportion in municipal expenditures might be caused by the fact that state owned enterprises still provide the service (for example the heating supply in Latvia).

This reduced budget share of public utility services could also mean that these services are more privatized and that they are less dependent on local budget transfers (for example Hungary). In most cases even the locally set user charges are not presented among the local budget revenues, because they are collected by the service organizations.

Fiscal information collected by the authors of the country reports also present the differences in terminology and data collection. However, the more detailed data from Hungary shows that in a decentralized system—when services are mostly provided by companies from arms length—local current and capital expenditures might be significantly different. Public utility services are high priority target areas of local capital investments (43% of total capital expenditures). Only 9% of local current expenditures used for the operation of utility services. According to our investigation, the modernization of urban services consists of the following main changes:

i)   decomposition of formerly monopolistic providers (re-structuring);

ii)   sale of assets and shares (privatization in a narrower sense) establishing liberalized market environment.

Different models have arisen in specific sectors of the studied countries, but there are common processes as well. Public utility and communal enterprises used to be owned by the state in former socialist systems. They were in monopolistic positions, although these monopolies were relatively weak in comparison to the state owned companies in the manufacturing sectors. It means that priorities in the development of public services only followed preferred ambitious political programs on the forced increase of production in heavy industry, mining, et cetera. Therefore, monopolies of public services were not really strong in relation to other sectors of the economy, but their behavior was typically monopolistic in their own sectors.

In most of the infrastructure sectors, service provision was divided among large enterprises, combining production, transmission, distribution and other related activities. Some activities were also connected to the basic services, like the operating of sport clubs, networks of social care institutions, financing a relatively wide range of exclusive services for employees, and so on.

Under these circumstances, the first step of transformation was the re-structuring of monopolies. Practically it meant the preservation of monopolies in another structure, in order to prepare them for real changes in the system of ownership and the establishment of the market environment. In the second stage of transformation, privatization is implemented in all of the possible service areas.

The content of these changes is different in the case of services according to their character as natural monopolies or mixed goods, because the role of public sector cannot be defined in the same way as in market economy. This difference is shown by Table 1.5.

The present changes of the public utility sector in countries of Central and Eastern Europe are parts of a longer process in the economic transformation. During the decades of state ownership and planned economy, the infrastructure and public services were secondary objectives. Industrial development, mostly in manufacturing and military sectors, was regarded as the primary goal of economic policy. This has supported the modernization of typically agrarian countries of the CEE region.

It has required extensive regrouping of available economic resources to the preferred activities and sectors. With the exception of some services (e.g. public education, urban housing) various mechanisms of the planned economy caused serious under-investment in the infrastructure services. In the centralized public administration and local government systems, the methods of allocating public utilities assisted the large scale industrial projects and did not respond to local needs and priorities. Extremely high income centralization has prevented any form of public choice based model of infrastructure financing.

Table 1.5

Stages of Transformation in Public Utility and Communal Services

	Public utilities (natural monopolies)	Communal services (mixed goods and services)
First stage (Re-structuring)	• modest breakup of state-owned monopolies (devolution of assets) • modest unbundling • establishment of independent regulatory authority	• rationalization • establishment of competitive environment
Second stage (privatization)	• privatization of competitive assets (de-monopolization) • development of regulatory function • liberalization	• de-monopolization • management of public shares • privatization

The past decade of transition raised the claim for dramatic changes in this field. The crisis of the Soviet economic rule coincided with the neo-conservative shift in economic policy. It has significantly changed the perception of public services and role of the government in service delivery. Separating the responsibilities of public service provision and the actual form of service production was the basic principle of reforms also in CEE countries. Various forms of privatization, together with new, decentralized forms of infrastructure financing have created a new environment for public utility services.

The lack of public funds for infrastructure development and the low level of public service performance raised the claim for a higher service efficiency, and the siphoning of more resources in this sector of the economy. Through the reallocation of internal sources and by attracting foreign direct investment, more funds were also made available in the local public utility sector. 'Municipalization' of state owned property of utility services, adaptation of new forms of private enterprises in service delivery, changing the rules of infrastructure financing through user charges and local taxation were the key elements of transformation. This process is still under implementation, as the studied countries started it at different moments and followed their own rules, which resulted diverging routes and speed of transformation.

4. RE-STRUCTURING SERVICE PROVISION

An indicator of structural changes in local public utilities is the scale and form of transforming the service organizations. According to the decentralization and privatization policies in a country, as a result of several transition waves, models are different also by sectors. In Table 1.6 a possible classification of organizational changes is summarized by sectors.

In the water services, three basic models were followed. In Hungary and Poland, the former large state owned and regional water works were fragmented, and several hundred small service organizations were created by local governments. The organizational forms are various: budgetary organizations, companies and private businesses provide water services. This model was not followed in Slovakia, where still a few state enterprises operate the water system and privatization is exceptional. Only the large and probably the best companies are taken by private investors. Romania has its own way by splitting the large national companies into semi-public forms of 'regie autonomes'.

District heating services were transferred to local governments in Hungary and Poland, which led to some privatization and slow amalgamation of these municipal service organizations. The other extreme case is Latvia, where heat production is still part of the national energy system and only a few cities have received the assets and set up their own company. This 'random municipalization' was combined with national government bail out of the indebted companies.

Transfer of public state property to local government, followed by privatization is most typical in municipal solid waste management. Local ownership is typical in several countries, slowly creating joint, economically rational size companies for waste disposal and collection. In Poland and Slovakia different methods are used for waste disposal and for collection: generally creating larger service organizations for disposal at regional level, whilst supporting competition in collection. In Slovakia, strong administrative measures were used for closing the sub-standard landfills.

Organizational models in communal services are determined by the country's characteristics and they are, in general, decentralized. In Hungary and Slovakia multi-purpose urban management service organizations were fragmented, by separating some revenue making and more market oriented activities from the rest. In Poland and Latvia, where the privatization of the social housing stock is lower, multi-profile companies provide combined services.

Table 1.6
Transformation of Service Organizations

WATER SERVICES
Extensive fragmentation   Hungary: 5 national and 28 regional water and sewage companies were dissolved to 5 state owned regional companies and 400 local government service organizations in 1991/92   Poland: 50 single purpose water enterprises (40 is managed by the regions) were fragmented. A survey in 1999 showed that water services are provided by 369 budgetary enterprises, 344 companies, 19 state owned enterprises, 10 budgetary entities.   *Changes in organizational forms*   Romania: by creating the regie autonomes, former SOEs were split among the county local governments, under semi-public forms of operation.   *Exceptional 'municipalization' and privatization*   Slovakia: 5 state, 2 local and 2 private companies, with a mandate to transfer them by December, 2001. (Similar process is followed in the Czech Republic, where the Prague water works had been recently privatized.)
DISTRICT HEATING
Transfer to local governments   Hungary: 290 local heat generation and distribution companies transferred to 103 local governments   Poland: 55 regional heat supply companies were transferred to app. 600 heat suppliers at 'gminas' (local authorities).   *National networks prevail, with random 'municipalitization'*   Latvia: exceptional, heavily subsidized privatization in a few cities (e.g. Riga, Jelgava)

Table 1.6 (continued)
Transformation of Service Organizations

MUNICIPAL SOLID WASTE MANAGEMENT
Transfer to local ownership, random privatization
Czech Republic, Hungary: Single municipality or joint local government service organizations. (Hungary: majority private ownership in 4% of sample cases).
Wide scale privatization in collection
Poland: in waste disposal 1 500 enterprise (600 corporations); collection is widely privatized (e.g. companies in Warsaw).
Slovakia: separating collection and landfill management, enforcing regionalization: 60% of 17 large regions are managed by private companies[15]

COMMUNAL SERVICES, HOUSING MANAGEMENT
Splitting multi-profile companies
Hungary, Slovakia: creating smaller units; sale or leasing, contracting arrangements; some exceptions for buying back companies (Slovakia)
Continuing multi-purpose communal companies
Poland: transforming to enterprises (gmina), 200 social housing associations operating independently
Latvia: local government companies, providing great variety of services indicate more frequent use of budgetary organizations, or more extensive fiscal transfers to municipal enterprises.

4.1 Re-structuring Communal Service Provision

The transformation process of service providers is similar, although stages having reached are different by countries and by sectors. Actual differences do not seem to lead to separate models. We suppose that the same process is going on, although different stages have been taken.

The first step is the rationalization of formerly state-owned enterprises. First of all, it means the clarification of public profiles and the separation of different supplementary activities. Practically, the number of employees are decreased in this phase, in some cases radically. The pressure to rationalization is derived from the crises of the transformation. Fiscal limits became hard both at the national and local levels.

Then, transformation of public enterprises to companies under the company law was implemented without ownership changes. 100% shares of local or other state actors were realized, as a pre-requisite to the following sale. At this stage, a system-specific event occurred: a search for adequate owners. In principle, there were different options as follows:

- direct sale by state property agencies, in a centralized manner;

- devolution of assets to local governments (in this case local authorities should transform their enterprises and budgetary units);

- creation of at least partial other owners by law, especially managers, employees.

At this stage of transformation rationalization was going on. In spite of the relatively stable structure of owners, performance expectations increased. It is difficult to measure outputs and outcomes, but there had been a decrease in improving service efficiency inputs (measured in the number of employees).

At the same time another phenomenon emerged, on the other end of contracting relationships. From different reasons, public clients are forced to strengthen the tendering process, even in those cases when their own company was selected. A competitive or quasi-competitive environment started to develop. It was a rather contradictory situation, because mechanism and practice were not developed properly. Neither rules, nor contracting techniques were prepared well or detailed enough [See Chapter Two, Ken Baar's study].

There were advantages and real dangers in this situation for future development. Obviously designing the competitive environment is very important, because it is one of the most important prerequisites of market development in public services. On the other hand, if some important details are missing in a regulated system, it easily discredits the competition. Without organizational guarantees, a prescribed process, and an implementation of rules—formal tenders may support only corruption and personal bias.

Communal group of urban services is a relatively market oriented area. The first phase of transformation was prepared quite well in the following stages, i.e. the incorporation of the private sector. However, public influence on urban services remained relatively wide, realized mostly through budgetary and direct linkages. Dependence from government measures remained almost unchanged at this stage.

4.2 Re-structuring Public Utility Service Provision

Compared to the public management of communal services, the transformation of public utilities is more complicated because of the natural monopoly characteristic of services. Transformation of urban utility services cannot be separated from the reorganization of other utilities, like telecommunication, energy supply, national public transport (railways, airways), et cetera.

However, development is necessary for economic modernization purposes, and governments are not in the position to finance and manage all the required capital investments. Furthermore, private and other additional resources might be directed only to a transformed system, where public and private functions are clearly separated. These constraints push the transformation process in these sectors as well.

Models followed by the investigated CEE countries are the same, although different stages are reached in each country and sector. Firstly, monopolies were broken up modestly, i.e. following regional boundaries of large service delivery areas. The measures used in different services were as follows:

- a structural reorganization of state enterprises by territorial administrative units (Romania);

- the devolution of assets to local governments (Hungary);

- a discussion on local government shares (water and sewage works in Slovakia, gas works in Hungary).

In the second step, regional enterprises are transformed to companies under the commercial law with 100% shares of the national or local governments. In the meantime ownership, management and regulatory functions are being separated, initiated by the national legislation. Among urban services the energy sector (electricity and gas supply), water and sewage services, and district heating were the relevant ones. It is common that local governments are involved to some extent in this process as owners, managers and regulators.

The most complicated element of this stage is *'unbundling'*, i.e. the disintegration of monopolistic organizations and the ordering of their confused roles, especially by separation of different private and public functions. It can be implemented by separating those segments of natural monopolies in service provision and the promotion of new entry and competition in areas, which potentially can be easily opened to competitors.

It is relatively rare to establish regulatory function in its final format in the stage of re-structuring. According to experiences, the required functions are known quite well, however guarantees are premature and the independent character of regulatory bodies is missing. The organizational requirements are as follows:

i) *Independence.* Independence would be necessary to realize public regulatory functions. Control and leadership of the regulatory organization should be based on different professional and social interests. The overall administrative influence of the government should be avoided. Involvement of different interest groups does not mean necessarily their direct representation in the management. It can be solved in other way, like regulation on specific rights of nomination, making regular Parliamentary reports, et cetera. The organizational model must not be integrated in the state administration or in the hierarchy of traditional subordination of government offices.

ii) *Separation of public regulator's functions.* The independent regulator's function should be separated from different other state tasks linked to the provision of public utility services. There are other roles influenced by state policies: taxation, urban planning, regional development, and so on.

iii) *Types of regulators.* Regulators usually operate at the central level. It is one of the most important guarantees of their independence from the state administration. Local governments may also be regulators of some local public services, like solid waste management, water and sewerage supply. However, this function is not separated from general local functions. In this case, institutionalization is involved in the development of the whole codification on local authorities. This solution can be criticized, because of the controlling influence of local politics.

4.3 Sequencing, Motives and Implementation

4.3.1   Sequencing Transformation

Based on the examples from the studied countries, there are four major stages of transforming the local public utility service organizations:

i) 'communalization', i.e. the transfer of state owned property to local governments. It is combined with some form of 'unbundling' (as previously described);

ii) 'corporatization', which is the transformation of the budgetary organizations to arms-length corporate entities, operating under the company law;

iii) 'privatization', by inviting foreign or domestic investors, attracting external capital in different forms of alternative service delivery (contracting out, concession, Build-Operate-Transfer {BOT});

iv) 'regulation' as a key precondition of full liberalization in the utility and communal sector.

These steps do not follow each other in this sequence, but they were used mostly in those countries which started decentralization in the early 1990s. In the unstable legal, political and financial environment methods of radical changes had to be developed and learned by all the participants. That is why sometimes deadlines were set for selecting the 'best' form of service organizations, which fits into the local political environment (e.g. in Hungary: 1996; in Latvia: 2002). Those countries where the decentralization process was slower, these steps do not necessarily follow each other in this sequence. However, there are chances, that in Latvia district heating privatization will be implemented in parallel to the transfer of assets to local governments or the Romanian 'regie autonomes' will keep their mixed, semi-public character in the future.

i) The first stage of transformation, when the monolith state enterprises were dismantled to relatively independent units is an important step towards realizing the efficiency gains of decentralization. Despite the lack of information on the transformation of local public service organizations, all the potential forms of 'unbundling' were implemented in the six studied countries. In the case of communal service organizations, and sometimes in public transportation only the accounts and functions were separated within the large entities. This helped the local governments to realize the total costs of services and to identify the subsidies needed for specific activities. Cross subsidies are still prevailing and they are widely used for minimizing corporate income tax burden.

The vertical separation of service organizations was typical in the energy sector, where local heat distributors (and sometime generators) were transferred to local governments. In the water sector, state owned enterprises still operate some parts of the national networks, but often the regional and urban companies are 'municipalized', i.e. they are transferred to local governments.

The Romanian 'regie autonomes' are examples of regional or horizontal unbundling, when specialized or multi-purpose companies provide services for one region. It may support competition, but less efficiently, when service organizations are vertically separated.

ii) Creating new entities under corporate law is the next significant stage of transformation. Both service providers, client local governments and service producers, and contracting organizations learn the new rules of management and control. They operate under quasi market conditions, when service performance indicators and forms of financing are more or less determined. Obviously with one or a limited number of local government owners and under the supervision of local councilors the service organizations are more directly connected to their clients, than in the case of privatization.

However, clear assignment of responsibilities could make this form of operation beneficial for both parties. Local governments and service users do not have to pay for the profit in the service charges for the private owners. Service companies with municipal support might be operated as market entities and their market position can be improved (for example by receiving guarantees from the owner local governments to capital investment loans).

iii) Real changes in economic incentives are expected only after privatization. Rules on the transfer of state ownership to local governments sometimes does not allow the privatization of networks, so only the operational assets can be used as municipal equity in the privatized companies. Local governments often keep the ownership of key components in service delivery (e.g. landfills in municipal solid waste management).

The impact of privatization on service delivery greatly depends on the contractual relationship between the client local government and the service contractor. Selection process of partners, performance specification, agreement on price setting, service monitoring and renegotiations are the key elements of this contractual relationship.

The obvious consequence of this sequential transformation, that these stages should be supplemented with stage (iv).

iv)   Regulation in a broad sense should include the rules how the market can be entered, what functions and responsibilities remain at the local governments and in what financial environment operate these service organizations. These components will be discussed later in this summary chapter.

4.3.2   Motives Behind Transformation

The pace and form of transforming the service organizations in local public utilities greatly varies in Central and Eastern Europe. Diversity can be explained partially by the differences in motives of policy makers. Here some of the most important general incentives are discussed briefly. This list is far from complete, but these arguments were most frequently used during the transformation process.

Primary reasons for transforming the traditional public service organizations to local, market oriented entities was the desire to increase the efficiency and to improve the quality of the local public utility services. In the early 1990s there was a strong belief in the CEE countries, that market based mechanisms are superior to the old rules of service delivery in public sector. Based on the strategic goal to cut back public expenditures, most of the public sector reforms were pushing the transformation of budgetary organizations to commercial entities and initiated own revenue raising by public service organizations.

The objective of decentralization and incorporation of public service institutions all served these long term goals. Critical conditions of implementation are significant investments in these very capital intensive sectors. It was obvious that without sufficient domestic resources and under very limited local government borrowing capacity, only foreign direct investments will provide sufficient funds.

Another factor for attracting foreign investors was the dramatic decline in the consumption of some public services. Especially in the water sector, where the under utilized network capacities have increased the unit costs, only further extension of services helped. For example, large sewage treatment plants without sufficient collection networks could have never reached their optimal size of operation. The deteriorated public service had to be reconstructed, which also required external resources.

Lessons from the Western European countries on privatization in the public sector, introduction of alternative service delivery arrangements and competitive tendering procedures showed that market conditions cannot be simulated, but implemented. The real market mechanisms will provide that legal and financial environment, which will encourage the professional investors to enter these countries. Privatization of service organizations was one solution for attracting external resources.

Parallel to privatization, innovative local governments and service company managers were capable of adapting those rules, which have forced the modernization of management techniques. Local governments started to create a competitive market environment by specifying performance criteria, establishing some forms of contractual relationship and especially by decreasing municipal subsidies together with the pressure to increase the role of user charges in financing utility services. In response, public utility companies were forced to introduce efficiency measures, lay-off personnel, invest in their equipment, improve their revenue administration and learn new management techniques. The emerging market environment improved efficiency also at those municipalities which did not launch privatization of local utility companies.

However, there were some arguments against wide scale privatization. It might lead to further deterioration of local government assets and could in fact increase the unemployment in the period of economic crisis. In many cases local governments are large employers and the overstaffed communal service and utility companies might be the first targets of staff reduction in the public sector. So local governments—which have legal or informal responsibilities for local economic development—were reluctant to make the employees of public service organizations redundant. As one obvious consequence of privatization was the dismissal of employees, these fears have delayed structural changes in the local public utility sector.

4.3.3   Characteristics of Implementation

Due to great differences in the legal and financial environment in these countries and the competing arguments for or against privatization of service organizations, the process of transformation has also showed some peculiarities. The implementation was characterized by compromises, forced by the national rules of privatization and also by political debates at local governments. In the following paragraphs four special characteristics of this transformation process will be described.

The rules of municipal ownership were most important factors influencing the organizational changes in the local public utility sector. In some countries (e.g. Hungary, Poland) the general principle of state owned property transfer was the separation of core assets and negotiable or enterprise property of local governments. The core property was those type of assets which are used for delivering basic public services and cannot be transferred or sold to businesses. Public utility networks are the best examples of this type of property. Other assets (equipment, machinery, buildings, et cetera) which are used in the operation of the core property were not controlled by the regulations on property transfer.

In other countries, where the ownership and control was stronger or the rules of property transfer were sometimes violated, the privatization process was distorted. A typical form of intervention was the involvement of national privatization agencies in the transformation of local public utility services. In the Czech Republic, where the state ownership dominates the water sector, the privatization deals are made by the State Property Agency. As the example of Prague shows, local governments are only invited to this decision making process, but they are in the minority (only two city representatives in an eight-member committee of the SPA, awarding the concession contract to the foreign service organization).

In Romania, even the local concession agreements have to be endorsed by a government decision, which requires the approval of the National Privatization Agency and the Ministry of Industry and Trade. The privatization of natural gas service in Hungary was also managed by the State Property Agency, which violated the rules of local property transfer. Municipal assets were sold to foreign service companies and local governments were compensated only several years later, following the decision of the Constitutional Court decision.

Lack of general rules on public utility services encourages preferential treatment of some forms of organizations and even sectors or cities. The purposes of these exceptional actions are usually to make the service organizations more attractive to investors. They are financed through public funds, which means that exceptions are made on the costs of general taxpayers.

In Romania since 1997 the incorporation of the 'regia autonome' was encouraged by a government emergency ordinance, which rolled back 60% of the potential privatization revenues to the new companies. It is mostly used for paying the debt of the 'regie autonomes', but it simply made the sale or concession cheaper for the investors. In Latvia the 'municipalization', and later privatization of the Riga district heating company was accompanied with significant national government bail out, because all the debt and arrears of the local unit of the national energy company was taken over by the remaining part of the state enterprise.

Legal forms of service companies also showed particularities in the CEE countries. Some form of local government public enterprises survived the economic changes for a limited period in several countries. For example in Hungary and Latvia, these special mixtures of not-for-profit commercial entities had to be transformed to legal entities under the budget or commercial law by a certain date. According to a survey, in Poland between 1993 and 1995 the share of these municipal enterprises in service delivery decreased from 19%; by 10% and at the same time proportion of budgetary organizations in service delivery increases by 4% and ratio of companies by 6%.

During the first years of transformation some forms of direct public ownership were also developed in the communal sector. Management buy outs and allocation of shares to company employees or to a foundation of employees were the typical instruments. This model was used in communal and housing management services in the case of Hungary and Poland. Employee's shares were always in minority (up to 5%), but they made the transformation acceptable for many local governments. Later these shares were sold or their influence was only symbolic.

The slowly emerging regulatory environment was supposed to influence the transformation process. In Latvia, the stated primary function of the future local regulators will be to take over the political burden of privatization from the elected local governments and to provide technical, financial arguments for privatization. In Hungary the introduction of compulsory competitive tendering in some sectors (e.g. municipal solid waste management) aimed to improve the service efficiency. It is another story as to how the general rules were violated, by saying, that competitive tendering should be used only under certain conditions: if the local government does not provide the service with its own service organization and only in the case of new contracts.

Price regulations also might have an impact on selecting the form of service provision, like in the case city of Komarno in Slovakia, where the 100% city owned service company shifted from a joint, sub-regional service management to a contractual relationship with the neighboring towns and villages. Under the regional model the water charges, set by the Ministry of Finance were equalized, so the city residents paid partially the more expensive service of the surrounding area. Under a contractual relationship each municipality pays a different price, based on its own costs and service performance.

Finally, a very recent characteristic is the appearance of political clientalism in the public utility service organizations. Local government ownership rights are accomplished through the appointment of company managers and the delegation of councilors to management and supervisory boards. Earlier these positions were taken by those councilors, who had some management or technical skills, but now they are mostly political appointees. Obviously there is no empirical evidence on this trend, but the issues discussed and the style of debates proves that it does exist.

This is another reason for improving the regulatory environment, before the strong local political influence destroys the efficiency gains in the transformed companies. It is especially important to have clear rules of conflict of interest and to regulate the councilors' compensation for participating in these boards. Otherwise there is the danger of forced amalgamation and stronger involvement of national state in the service management.

5.   PRIVATIZATION AND REGULATION

After these preparations, the privatization is the second stage of transforming urban services. Privatization is the key phenomenon of economic transition in the CEE region. When analysts compare different countries, they focus on models of privatization followed by particular regimes [Kornai, 2000]. In local public utility sectors, speed and radicalism of privatization are not discussed, because changes only follow the manufacturing sectors. The limits to privatization are also different, because some public functions remain. Privatization of natural monopolies and mixed services is implemented through different actions, including the transformation of the economic environment. Three basic components will be discussed here:

1) The searching for real owners;

2) The establishment of a competitive environment;

3) The development of public regulatory functions.

5.1 Searching for Real Owners

Seeking real owners was the strategic goal of the general privatization model, primarily followed by Hungary and Poland. Other solutions in the business sector, like the voucher based privatization were mainly preferred in the Czech Republic. Out of the group of countries investigated in our analysis it was also typical in Russia. In urban services this model was not widespread, presumably, because of technical reasons.

i) *Mixed Goods and Services*

In the case of mixed urban goods (communal services) a model of small-scale privatization could be followed. Formerly local monopolies are attempted to divide these services into smaller units and give to private ownership. Typically park maintenance services, road maintenance, public cleaning, solid waste removal, individual liquid waste removal, and so on, was reorganized in this way.

Methods of small-scale privatization are various. Most typical forms are as follows:

- selling to managers (especially former budgetary units, and enterprises);

- re-privatization/restitution (formerly social housing sector in Czech Republic, Slovakia);

- right to buy (selling social dwellings to sitting tenants, e.g. in Hungary);

- sale of assets or shares (like profitable companies dealing with road maintenance, etc.).

In some cases, public functions are eliminated by the privatization, in others responsibilities remain public to some extent. For instance, provision of park maintenance remains a local responsibility even if private firms implement it. With re-privatization or sale to sitting tenants of formerly state-owned dwellings, municipalities reduce most of maintenance costs. Finding owners seems to be easier in these sectors in most of the CEE countries, that is why reorganization was more flexible here than in other utility services.

ii) *Natural Monopolies*

Public utility services as natural monopolies are subjects of large-scale privatization. Generally speaking large-scale privatization means breaking monopolies of large state-owned firms and giving them into private property.[16] This step can be made at least in two ways. One is to transfer assets to private property without any crucial changes. In this case state-owned property is transferred to private monopoly, for example in Russia in the energy sector, including gas and electricity.

The other route is to transfer to competitive companies, whilst preserving necessary public functions under the public control. It is more complicated, requires political commitment, along with more time and conception. Problems and conflicts are shown by the reluctance in changes. In most of the countries there are sectors which remained under state supervision for the time being. However, the speed does not seem to be crucial. More important is the specification of the development. 'Unbundling', as a necessary step is going ahead in a quite conflicting way. National governments are reluctant to diminish their influence. For different reasons it is more attractive to preserve state positions, as directing authority or at least as owner of majority shares.

5.2 Establishment of Competitive Environment

The biggest challenge of restructuring is if a competitive environment does not emerge in the region. It seems to be a real problem, when formerly state-owned monopolies are transferred to private monopolies. Even if they are international ones, as soon as they get strong positions on the market, they are not interested any more in the further market-oriented development. Their usual argument is that modernization of utility services requires a high level of capital investments, financed by companies having preferential status and temporarily enjoying higher returns.

Sometimes, national governments are also counter-interested in real changes after the first phases of transformation. The momentum of modernization is sufficient for the denationalization of public services in a mechanic way (i.e. simply transferring to private monopolies, or more typically supplementing state positions with private monopoly interests). After this there is no real motivation to continue the development of a competitive market. Monopoly interests and other motivation of particular interest groups for a short period are against the strong competition.

An interesting example is the Hungarian one, where the national government influenced price setting in gas and electricity sectors. It was implemented without any negotiations with market actors, increasing the disapproval of investors and service providers of these clear (social) policy motivations. Consequences of this government decision were clearly certified by the stock exchange.

This influence was made possible because of the purely functioning regulatory body and with the help of the crucial (golden) share of the state in the remaining monopoly gas production company and state-owned electric transmission company. Energy plants, distributors in the electric and gas sector have already been privatized and competitors have been on the market. However, transferring grid and distribution remained monopolized, and it was sufficient to anti-market influence.

Similar tendencies have arisen in communal services in the CEE region. Local governments, as public actors, are not in an equal position with other clients in many respects. Their influence on policy formation is not institutionalized to the necessary extent, freedom of choice is quite uncontrolled. It means that effectiveness of service provision is not the primary criterion for local decisions. Elected bodies may be motivated by other reasons than public interest, sometimes by the councilor's own private ones. The transparency and publicity of local decisions are not effective enough to force local decision makers to follow unwritten or formal rules. These circumstances are against the emergence of a real competitive environment of public service provision.

A competitive environment can emerge in different phases and forms. In the case of communal services the process is relatively simple, because of the break up of former monopolies easily creates a favorable environment for competition. Local governments are dealing with several, almost equal actors for organizing and managing service delivery. A great variety of alternative service delivery forms (contracting out, management contracts, franchises, et cetera) helps them to use market incentives and also to create legal, financial environment for competition.

The situation is more complicated in the utility sector. Firstly, active liberalization policy is needed. Secondly, liberalization might not follow the privatization, because huge costs of modernization should be financed by guaranteed high returns. In this case, the establishment of competitive environment is implemented in a specific way, with the help of a conscious policy to open the markets. Liberalization can be achieved by opening the access to networks, or by eliminating temporarily accepted monopolies.

According to research carried out for this report, privatization is a more complex process in the utility sector than simply shifting from public ownership to another form of dominating property. Preconditions for market competition are as important as the transformation of ownership. Active policies are required for establishing the market environment, by allowing different actors to enter the market.

However, the process does not end with privatization and liberalization. Special features of the utility sector, described as market and government failures, further special regulatory functions should be established for ensuring sustainable development.

5.3 Regulation

5.3.1   Regulatory Concepts: Conflicting Areas

The term 'regulation' is used in a broad sense in the local public utility sector of Central Eastern European countries. It covers all the different pieces of legislation and various forms of government intervention, which influence the behavior of market entities. Based on the approaches and attitudes learned during the former decades of state ownership regulation, it includes more activities than the traditional forms of regulation like licensing, setting technical standards, taxation and planning, price regulation, and so on.

It is also used for elements of competition rules, like the prohibition of collusion, review of mergers, tendering and procurement procedures, providing third party access to networks, defining forms and specification of contracts, et cetera. These competition rules are used in both cases of competition: when companies compete for the market and when they are already rivals in the same market.

The third block of regulatory practices is the other forms of intervention for protecting the public interest. They are the government capital investment policies (grants, loans, guarantees), social policy subsidies, measures for customer protection and other ways of interference on the market.

All these three components of regulation are very much influenced by the privatization practices of the studied countries. Privatization has two interpretations in countries of Central and Eastern Europe. Sometimes the transfer of state owned property to autonomous local governments is regarded as privatization, even if this is a shift from one type of public ownership to another one. (This is the case in Latvia (e.g. water, district heating), where decentralization meant significant change from the soviet rule to a diverse and deconcentrated system.)

Another level of privatization, when local governments have some discretion over their newly gained property, but their autonomy to exercise ownership rights is limited. (For example the privatization of Prague waterworks was implemented by the national property fund, only with the involvement of the city officials, who were in minority during the decision making process.) A transitory form of privatization is when the transferred state property unit should be operated as an incorporated entity, as an organization under the company law. Under these schemes the service organization is managed and controlled like a real business entity, but the only shareholder is one public body.

The other interpretation of privatization is slowly developed, when real private owners take over the public service delivery organizations. Their share is dominant in the company, long term profit motivation is behind the investors actions. Social policy considerations are separated from the operational efficiency objectives.

This gradual development of regulatory mechanisms was influenced by the trend of legislative changes in the transition countries. The first step after the political transformation was the design and approval of a new constitution. Under the multi-party political system, in the transition towards a market economy, the basic principles had to be revised. The redesign of the local government act was part of this constitutional process. In this first period most of the countries set the basic concepts in company and privatization laws, even if the economic transition was started later.

49

The second wave of the legislative process was longer, and raised all those detailed questions, which were not clarified by the basic laws. The most important pieces of legislation for the local public utility sector were the fiscal and sectoral laws. They have identified the new forms of intergovernmental fiscal relations, expenditure and revenue assignment, forms of subsidies, price setting authority in public services, budgeting rules and procedures, forms and competencies of budgetary organizations. This was accompanied with the general economic legislation, when the competition rules, public procurement procedures, customer protection regulations were defined. Another broad and long process was the redesign of the various sectoral laws. In a decentralized public sector, under market conditions, the rules of managing water, solid waste, district heating and other services had to be modified. Not only the technical standards and actors have changed, but new concepts and procedures had to be built into the sectoral laws (e.g. identifying who is the waste producer: the municipality in Slovakia, or the citizens in Hungary). This sometimes required a rather long legislative process, because the new laws did not fit into the slowly transforming institutional environment. For example in Hungary, the law on waste management was debated for almost five years, because various governments and the Parliament were not in agreement as to how detailed the legislation should be, who should take the burden of higher technical standards, and so on.

This complex legislative process took sometimes a decade to come about, and due to political shifts and changes in concepts, it still today has not been completed in several countries. For example, the privatization of the Latvian energy company was refused by a referendum; whilst the volume based method of setting waste collection charges, required by several constitutional court decisions was made compulsory only by the Act on Waste Management several years later in Hungary.

As these different pieces of legislation are not always harmonized, the broad regulatory environment is sometimes contradictory. The principles laid down by the constitution and local government acts are not always in line with the general rules of competition and tendering. The local governments prefer to set exceptional rules for their own service organizations, while the public procurement and tendering regulations treat all the economic entities equally. This has raised conflicts, for example in Hungary and Latvia, where municipalities wanted preferential treatment of their own service organizations. Another typically argued area is price setting, where the economic principle of full cost recovery and social policy considerations are always opposing. The third broad area of legislation, the sectoral laws, have also raised several conflicts. As sector specific laws are designed by the relevant ministries, which can be more easily influenced by lobby organizations, and they often reflect the interests of the large service organizations. Line ministries claim more responsibility for these service organizations, which were even 'owned' and managed by the central administration a decade earlier, under the system of state ownership. One example is the Hungarian municipal waste regulation, which—under some conditions— requires the compulsory use of communal grants for compensating the losses of service organizations, originated from uncollected user charges. Often safety and stability of services is protected by these sectoral laws, creating tension with the principles of local autonomy and general rules of economic competition and market behavior.

5.3.2   Elements of Regulation

Following the broad interpretation and use of regulation, the most important components will now be briefly discussed. They influence local public utility service delivery to a different degree, but our purpose is to identify all the relevant elements of regulation. Without this inventory, the present status of regulatory mechanisms in the studied countries of Central Eastern Europe cannot be understood. These components are as follows:

a)   Legislation on organizational forms and taxation rules;

b)   Licensing, service permits;

c)   Sectoral planning and strategic decision;

d)   Capital investment financing schemes;

e)   Contracting and tendering regulations;

f)   Setting user charges and prices of the service;

g)   Forms of consumer protection.

These seven groups of tools and instruments cover the major types of regulatory means. Their significance is different for local public utilities and for communal services. The scale of government influence is also different by services. Licensing, price setting, and consumer protection is more important for the widely privatized services; while planning, capital investment financing and contracting is the typical way of influencing services closely connected to local governments. Obviously the techniques also vary by sectors: for example price setting methods are not identical for the network based monopolistic services and in sectors with high competition and contracting out practices.

a)   Legislation on Organizational Forms

Organizational forms of local public utility service delivery are similar in all these countries. These services might be produced by the local administration (departments) or by different forms of budgetary organizations. These local government institutions are under the control of local governments, but their property rights and autonomy in managing their own finances are different. They are usually part of the local budget, except in Slovakia, where the 'contributory organizations' establish a net fiscal relationship with the municipal budget. In this case they collect own revenues, enjoy higher discretion in employment and they are allowed to keep the operational surplus.

A mixed form of operation is the 'municipal enterprise', which are public sector entities, but have some characteristics of businesses. This was a typical solution for transferring the former state owned companies to local governments, whose possibilities as owners were limited. Sometimes these organizations were transitional forms, when a deadline was set by the national legislation for deciding whether they will operate as budgetary or as business entities. (This was the case in Hungary, where these 'inherited' enterprises were forced to be transformed by 1996, or in Latvia, where the companies in the energy sector have to be transformed by 2002).

In Romania the 'regie autonomes' operate in natural monopoly services, with high capital investment needs, where competition can be developed only in the long run. They are legal entities under the public law and in the case of corporatization, their assets must be recorded separately. In the case of privatization, only the management functions and not the assets can be transferred to new owners under concession agreements. Most of the water, communal waste, and district heating services are provided by these special mixed organizations.

The third group of service organizations are the business entities under the company law. They are the traditional forms of joint-stock companies, limited liability companies, partnerships or some forms of public purpose (not-for-profit) companies. They might be owned exclusively by the local governments, or by different owners, under different proportions of shares.

These three groups of service organizations operate under different taxation and accounting rules (e.g. depreciation rates, VAT rules are different according to their legal status). In the energy sector the bookkeeping rules are also different, because as a first step towards 'unbundling', the costs and revenues of generation, transmission and distribution are reported separately (for example Poland). Countries, such as Poland, with a significant local social housing stock provide preferential treatment for housing management companies. Here, construction and reconstruction is subsidized through PIT allowances and reduced VAT rates for building materials.

Generally in all countries, there are expectations towards some mixed forms of service delivery organizations. Arguments for combining profit and public motives are social policy considerations, cross subsidization of loss making activities, higher grants from local governments for operation and capital investment projects. These expectations are usually not met and obviously all the benefits of clear profit motivation are lost under these schemes. So despite the higher service costs in a for profit company, the efficiency gains and better service quality in these capital intensive sectors are the advantages of the business companies.

Data on company forms in some selected sectors (water, solid waste management, district heating) are based on surveys. Information from these samples is not really comparable, but it shows some country particularities. For example, in Hungary the most typical service organizations in the solid waste and water management sectors are government enterprises (44% of the total number of service organizations) and budgetary institutions (38%). In Latvia, local government institutions are the most frequent operational forms (52% in the water sector and 37% of solid waste management units).

In Slovakia, where only aggregate numbers are available, local service organizations with 100% municipal ownership are mostly budgetary organizations (72%) and companies are less frequently used (28%). When several local governments run joint businesses, they prefer limited liability companies (55%) or joint-stock companies (42%). The rest of the service organizations are partnerships and cooperatives. In Romania, out of the approximately 400 service operators 'regie autonomes' (35%) and companies (35%) are the most frequent organizational forms; but in-house units are also widely used (30%). 'Regie autonomes' serve

Table 1.7
Legal Forms of Service Organizations

Hungary	Budgetary institutions	Companies	Private Entrepreneur	Other	Total
Municipal solid waste, water services	38%	44%	11%	7%	100%

Latvia	LG Institution	LG Enterprise	State Enterprise	Joint Stock Co., Ltd.	Private Persons	Total
Water sector (N=300)	52%	28%	3%	9%	8%	100%
Solid waste management (N=300)	37%	22%	3%	28%	10%	100%

Romania	In House Units	Companies	Regie Autonomes	Total
N=app. 400 units	30%	35%	35%	100%

Slovakia	Budgetary Organizations	Companies	Total
Exclusive local government ownership	72%	28%	100%
	Joint Stock Companies	Limited Liability Companies	Partnerships	Cooperatives	Total
Joint local ownership	42%	55%	2%	1%	100%

SOURCE: LGPP country reports, DFID-LGI, 2001

the largest proportion of the population (70%), as they are mostly organized at the 'judet' (county) level.

Local public utility services are operated under various legal forms. Both public and clear private entities are present, but some mixed forms have also survived. They and the public institutions give wider competencies and more options for influencing the local public utility services. This regulatory authority is more indirect and general in the case of business companies.

b)   Licensing

For providing local public utilities, any type of the above mentioned service organizations should go through the licensing process. Permissions are based on various pieces of sectoral legislation: technical standards, environmental protection requirements; employment rules; and financial criteria supplement the service licenses. Some areas of these sectoral regulations are more developed, as traditionally they were subjects of legislation: for example in Hungary, which is geographically located in a basin, regulations on the water management standards are more matured than the rules of other services.

There are also new fields of licensing process, for example the energy sector, after the privatization and devolution of some responsibilities to local governments. District heating is an example which should fit into the changing institutional environment. Based on the example of the Hungarian law on district heating, the following new elements of service regulations were set (similar elements of regulation are specified by the Act on Energy in Slovakia).

First of all, the competencies of the central and local governments have to be specified. They should be harmonized with the requirements of consumer protection, involving such components as: access to information; justification of costs; managing complaints, and so on. Conditions for the issuing of licenses of heat generation are regulated in great details, specifying also the rights and duties related to heat transmission and grid ownership. A contractual relationship has to be established between the heat generators and the transmission, distribution companies on one hand and between the distribution companies and the customers on the other hand. Critical elements of this relationship are the metering, restriction on service delivery and payments of user charges.

It is a different issue as to how these new rules are enforced, which level of government and under what organizational form, lies the responsibility of the implementation. Typically, sector oriented regulatory bodies are established. Models will be discussed later, but the example of energy supply shows three basic methods.

The most centralized form is when a central government unit (ministry) is responsible for the regulation (e.g. Ministry of Economy in Slovakia). In other countries, independent regulatory agencies were established with a great variety in their rights and competencies. In Romania, the regulatory agency is involved in the design of an energy policy (price setting, allocation of subsidies, and so on), so it is closer to the actual government. In Hungary and Poland, the regulatory agencies enjoy greater independence from the political influence of the government. Finally the most decentralized system of 'local regulators' has been set up recently in Latvia, even before the real privatization of the energy sector was started.

Control of other local public utility services is organized according to the public administration system of a given country. These regulatory and licensing functions might be part of the higher (intermediary) tiers of sub-national government, which also implement central public administration functions (districts, regions). In other countries, local and regional units of central government agencies are responsible for licenses, control of technical standards and procedures (decentralized units of water, environmental, public health agencies).

c)   Planning

Beside licensing and permit procedures, there are other ways and indirect means of influencing local public utility services. Depending on the scope of decentralization, different levels of local governments are responsible for the planning and strategy design. Local government environmental protection programs (affecting municipal solid waste management, communal services, and so on), plans for energy and heating supply, water sector development strategies are the most direct forms of influence. They might be assigned to lowest level of elected local governments or hierarchical relationship exists between municipal and regional government plans and strategies.

Other public utility services are designed as a part of the physical planning process. Land use planning is the most obvious form of local planning competencies, which has an impact on public utilities. They might create favorable conditions for the development of public utility services.

d)   Capital Investment Financing

Without sufficient financial resources, these planning competencies have only a limited influence on public utility services. There are various capital investment financing schemes in each studied countries, providing funds for those local capital investment projects, which are in line with the national development policies.

The most targeted forms of capital grants are designed and allocated by the central budget. The Public Investment Program in Latvia (3–5% of GDP), or earmarked subsidies from the central budget to local investment projects (e.g. in Romania) are traditional forms of capital grants. In a more decentralized local government structure targeting is achieved through matching grants schemes (e.g. in Hungary, where municipal water projects and solid waste landfill construction are subsidized in 30–40% of the total investment costs; their share is usually 5% of local budgets).

Other preferred forms of allocating targeted subsidies are the funds and special appropriations, managed by sectoral ministries. They might be controlled by the general budgetary policy or often they enjoy greater independence as separate funds, allocated by the relevant ministries (e.g. water management, environmental protection, transportation). The amount and spending of extra-budgetary funds are obviously controlled by the national fiscal policy (Ministry of Finance) to a lesser degree than subsidies through other centralized appropriations. On the other hand, they support sectoral development policies and programs more efficiently. Often these sectoral ministries manage and allocate the subsidies through international donor and assistance programs. These sources of capital investment might be significant in the EU accession countries under various environmental and regional development programs.

In the period of economic decline, when demand for capital investment in public utility services is high and increasing, there is a need for external funding. They might be provided through national budget loan schemes or ensuring direct access to international financial institutions and commercial banks. Local government borrowing is controlled through various schemes. Before 1999, local governments in Romania were allowed to borrow on the international finance markets only after obtaining government approval. In Latvia, a special borrowing council evaluates specific municipal projects financed by loans. The limit of local government borrowing is set by the annual budget. In other countries like Hungary, there are only general rules on local government debt burden (and issued guarantees), set in percentage of total own source revenues. Here also, the procedures of local government bankruptcy are set by law, this way avoiding the national government bail-outs and improving the financial discipline of local decision makers.

Other indirect forms of supporting local government borrowing also exist in some countries in local public utilities. In Latvia special guarantees are issued for local utility company loans to a very limited scale (one or two cities per year). Some international lending organizations require a sovereign guarantee issued by the national government. This is a widely used technique in Romania, but to a lesser degree in countries where local governments have easier access to international financial markets (Hungary, Poland). Besides guarantees, national governments may influence local capital investments through specific interventions like the writing off municipal debts or not claiming dividends on their shares (e.g. Latvia).

Modern forms of public-private partnership schemes in local utility services are less developed than in the studied countries. Concessions are the only widely used techniques, but not all the local public utility services fit into framework of concession laws. Other BOT (Build-Operate-Transfer) techniques are slowly developing, partly because of underdeveloped banking services, lack of professional experiences and management capacity on the local governments' side and sometimes because of incomplete local regulatory environment (e.g. price setting, forms and scale of owners' influence).

e)   *Competition Rules*

Contracting and tendering for public contracts are parts of the broad regulatory framework. In typical cases, public contracts are made between the local government entitled to provide the service and the service producers. Here, the local government as a public authority establishes a contractual relationship with the service organization. It might be even an in-house unit or any arms-length entity, partly or entirely independent from the municipality. Content and format of these contracts are regulated mostly by sectoral laws or in specific cases (like the concession agreement) by separate laws. Contracts are also made between the customers and service producers, which are mostly regulated by the civil code (water services, district heating, waste collection, etc.).

This raises the first problem, whether the citizens should accept the service organization, selected and designated by the local government. In the case of Hungary where citizens have the technical possibility to choose among different service producers (for example municipal solid waste management, or chimney sweeping) the mandatory use of the service was set by the law. So the citizens have to use the benefits of the locally organized service (that is, they have to pay for it) and the contracts have to be signed with that specific service organization, as selected by the local government.

Other problems of the contracting process were related to tendering and public procurement. The basic principle of the tendering regulations is that if public contracts are made, then the general rules of public procurement have to be followed. This rule is often under pressure or not adhered to, because formally the contract is signed between the individual customer and the service organization assigned by the local government. Formally, no public money is used during the contract, because customers pay directly to the service organization. This gives various misinterpretations of the public procurement rules. The fact is that in this relationship, the local government acts on behalf of all the local citizens and represents the community.

Another argument against the use of public procurement rules is that the local government as the shareholder of a service company or founder of a budgetary institution is limited in the use of its own property. That is why public procurement and tendering regulations are interpreted differently even in the same country. Consequently following the hierarchy of laws, the transparency and efficiency requirements of the public sector supersedes the demand of public entities to exercise their own property rights.

Public contracts should be awarded through public tenders. These rules are already developed in all the studied countries. Public procurement legislation was among those new laws, which were approved in the early stage of preparing a developed market environment. Following the international standards subjects, thresholds of public procurement and procedures were set. Public entities, including local governments and their budgetary institutions have to follow the general procurement rules.

Value limits of public procurement in all the three categories of purchase (goods, services, construction works) are usually lower in the CEE region than in other countries. The value limits are developed parallel to public procurement and tendering rules. Organizational forms show great variety: the Czech Competition Protection Authority operates as a central government agency, the Latvian Purchase Supervision Bureau is under the Ministry of Finance, while the Hungarian Public Procurement Council is appointed by and reports to the Parliament.

It is frequently debated whether municipal companies, using public funds, are forced to follow the public procurement rules or not. The general principle of public procurement would claim the broad interpretation of tendering obligations, so any subsidiaries of local governments have to use the tendering regulations. In local practice this is not the case.

Another problem is that public utility services are usually not mentioned by the public procurement acts. If the sectoral laws do not specify the tendering requirements, then local governments escape from the strict tendering and contracting rules. This has a disadvantageous impact on service efficiency and transparency of local governments.

f)   Price Formulation

Price setting is the critical component of the regulatory system. In the market environment. user charges should reflect the total costs of the service, and at the same time should signal the demand for the public utility service. Both of these requirements were new for these countries, where consumer prices were heavily subsidized, and service companies were compensated for their lower revenues. Social policy considerations determined the price levels and preferences, so they did not indicate the real needs for a particular service.

During the transformation of public utility sector each country went through a similar process, only the speed of changes was different. The basic factor behind these changes was the cut in state and other government subsidies on public utility services. In some countries, this was accompanied with the decentralization of price setting competencies, parallel to the devolution of service ownership and management functions.

The present price setting authority follows the characteristics of utility services. The more connected the service provision to networks and the greater chances of monopolies, the more regulated and centralized is the method of price setting. User charges are often defined as official prices, calculated at different levels of government. The greatest chances of centralized price setting are in the energy sector (district heating). In Latvia, Poland, and Romania, user charges of district heating are defined by the central energy regulatory agencies, mostly after consultation with the competition offices or boards.

District heating is the subject of subsidies for example in Romania, where the 'national reference price' is set for the customers. This is driven by the costs of the large national energy companies and it is accompanied with a subsidy to local governments, where the local price is above the national reference price.

The basic problem of the energy sector and the related local utility services is that because of the declining industry, consumption is also decreasing (e.g. in Latvia use of energy was decreased by 40% in the period of transition). In this sector, where the fixed costs are relatively high, declining consumption will lead to increasing unit costs. Due to the capital intensive production, amortization, replacement and maintenance costs remain high, even if the consumption is decreasing.

Price setting mechanisms and related regulatory institutions are also underdeveloped in the region. Prices are approved or controlled by some national agencies (ministries and boards), but they are usually calculated on a cost based method. Modern techniques of price capping, or profit rate regulations with some exceptions (e.g. Hungary) are not introduced. This fact does not support privatization and structural changes in the energy sector. Government subsidies and various forms of 'bail out' still exist. All these factors have an unfavorable impact on those local utility services, which are dependent on or part of the energy sector.

The privatization effort in the Latvian capital city district heating system is a clear example of these bad practices. The assets of Riga district heating company was first separated from the national energy company. Some of the heat generators and the distribution network created the basis of a local company. Obviously it was loaded with significant debt, because of the high arrears, but this debt was taken over by the national energy company, which meant practically a government withdrawal. It was followed by the privatization, improving the quality of the service and efficiency of the company. Because of the exceptional character of this privatization process, no other municipalities were able to follow the example of the capital city.

In the energy sector, the decision on the consumer's 'ceiling price' (maximum price) (in Slovakia) or 'reference price' (in Romania) involves the definition of two other component of prices. The setting of production prices by heat generators is a part of the process and consequently subsidies are also specified during these negotiations. This is partly based on the technical specifications of the sectoral (energy) laws, partly influenced by social policy and welfare payment systems (e.g. what type of benefits and how they will compensate for the price increase). Problems fall back on service organizations, when subsidies do not cover the difference between the producer price and the maximized consumer prices (e.g. this happens often in countries with a high level of social housing stock, where the condominiums and housing cooperatives cannot enforce payments of tenants).

Depending on the system of public administration, user charge setting competencies might be decentralized to a lower level of government. In Slovakia, where the district offices operate as non-elected, state administrative units, in most cases public utility service prices are set by them. The Ministry of Finance determines a range of services, where price calculation is the mandate of district offices. These maximum prices are set "in consultation with the municipalities" and several other organs of state administration are involved in this process (e.g. Office of Financial Control, Slovak Trade Inspection). District offices define prices of district heating, water and sewage, waste disposal, public transport, parking services, et cetera.

In a decentralized Hungary, the price setting authority of the central state was transferred to local governments in the early 1990s. Within the general framework of price formulation and anti-monopoly regulations ('Prohibition of Unfair Market Practices') local governments set the official prices of public utility services. So prices of water supply and sewage treatment, district heating local public transport are calculated through administrative procedures. User charges of communal waste management, chimney cleaning, services in public cemeteries as official prices are regulated by local government statutes.

These price setting methods are influenced by the broader economic environment. Primarily the cutback in national government and local subsidies forced the changes in service financing. There are some generally accepted principles of price calculation which also have to be followed. Based on the 'equality of services rendered and prices paid' principle, volume based pricing has to be accepted. This excludes sometimes the differentiation among various groups of customers. It may also increase the costs of the service, if the metering is expensive.

The design of user charges is highly influenced by the metering techniques and the possibilities for cost allocation among different customers. Large social housing estates were built in the era of subsidized low public utility services, when individual metering and control of individual consumption was not required. In these housing blocks, options for installing metering equipment is expensive or technically not feasible. The old one-pipe district heating systems need huge investments for redesigning, and tenants of these social apartments cannot afford the installation of any type of metering equipment (for example individual meters and cost allocation devices). Methods of price setting and the calculation of price increase are usually regulated. They are typically cost based techniques of designing user charges (cost factors are weighted and extrapolated according to generally accepted principles and reflected by agreed multipliers). Sometimes general principles are followed: "prices should cover the costs and profits of efficient service providers", in the case of energy prices in Hungary. In Poland a general rule is centrally set for regulating the municipal rents, which should not exceed annually the 3% of replacement costs.

Another basic problem is the price setting policies. The inherited practice of user charge setting is that individual customers are subsidized and large users of bulk services pay higher prices of energy. This prevailing practice has built wrong incentives into the energy sector and into the related local utility services. For example, consumers enjoying lower gas prices opt out of the large district heating systems more easily, because they compare their future investment and maintenance costs at a subsidized level of natural gas. This is frequently used in Romania (30% of users opted out from the local heating network and installed their individual systems), but also in other countries with extended district heating system (for example Latvia and Hungary). Local governments are simultaneously the owners and regulators of municipal utility services. In addition, councilors as local politicians are faced with social problems created by decreasing subsidies and transformation of utility services. These three conflicting functions also create tensions in the local price setting decision.

However, the price formulation function is an emerging and efficient component of regulation. The assignment of the price setting authority, allocation of competencies to influence the methods of designing user charges, is part of the public administration and local government reform process.

g) Protecting Customers

Demand for consumer protection was raised immediately after the traditional state institutions lost their influence on production and service provision. When organizations 'protecting the public interest' did not exist any more and the private property became the dominant form of the economy, new forms of consumer protections had to be designed. Several new areas of legislation provided basic conditions for supporting the consumer's relations to producers. Anti-monopoly and competition laws, acts of price setting, and contracting regulations are all passive ways to ensure a balanced relationship between buyers and providers of a service. Some additional general requirements on goods and services (e.g. labeling) were also part of the newly formulated consumer protection acts in all the studied countries in the very early 1990s.

In the area of public utility services and contracts, there is a need for more active forms of consumer protection. For example, free access to information is a critical condition for protecting the consumer's rights, when local public services are contracted by the municipal. Also customers should be involved in the regulatory process, when service standards, conditions and prices are determined.

In most of the studied countries, some institutions for consumer protection have survived at a national level. They might be independent agencies like the Consumer Protection Chief Inspection (Hungary), Office for Protection of Competition and Consumers (Poland), Bureau of Protection of Consumers (Latvia), or belong to a ministry, like the Commercial Inspection (Slovakia), Czech Commercial Inspection reporting to Ministry of Commerce and Industry.

In some sectors the regulatory agencies might have a stronger influence on service provision, so they indirectly have more means to protect consumer rights. Especially in the case of district heating, energy regulatory agencies are involved in price setting, which is the critical component of consumer-producer relationship. In Hungary, the public utility contract is also subject to the consumer protection procedure.

There are other decentralized forms of consumer protection, which can influence public utility service provision. Consumer Associations in Slovakia, or the tenant association in Latvia might be involved in the specification of service performance and conditions. Local government associations also play a role in these negotiations (for example in Latvia they are represented in the energy council), or the newly established system of 'local regulators' in Latvia is also an attempt to decentralize the problems and solutions of consumer protection.

Another question is what means are available for consumer protection agencies to enforce their clients' interest. Generally legal procedures, in some cases penalties and fines, are the only available measures. They are not a very efficient means for influencing specific actions of the service producers.

5.4 National Regulatory Functions

Independent regulatory function is one of the most important element of public roles under market circumstances. In theory, independence and autonomy have two dimensions: regulatory mechanisms should be exempt from the influence of public (state) administration and also from the pressure of large service producers, often being in a monopolistic position. The interpretation of autonomous regulatory organizations is even more confused, because in many respects the interest of bureaucracy is similar to private monopolies. That is why other public actors should be also involved in key policy decisions.

In CEE countries the first steps have been made by the establishment of regulatory organizations. There are experiments to build into their structure some elements of independence from the administrative structures. However, these are quite weak solutions. Practically, most of the existing regulatory institutions are traditional offices, subordinated to the administrative hierarchy, rather than public bodies with autonomy for policy formulation in particular sectors.

Local governments might also be in a regulatory position. But without sufficient guarantees, the decentralization of regulatory functions is questionable. The only positive example might be the Latvian one (see Chapter 5). The newly introduced legislation on local regulators seems to be the most developed one, hoping to establish a real independent regulatory organization at a local level.

Without independent authorities, necessary controls over natural monopolies is hard to imagine. Guarantees must be established, for instance by controlling the entry to the market. It is one of the techniques for supervising providers by limiting their harmful monopoly aspirations. In the case of unintended influence of authorities, public control may be transferred to state organs, that is to another type of monopoly. Then, instead of an independent public regulation, nationalized bureaucratic administration governs this important task.

Regulation in the narrow sense covers certain aspects of service provision: licensing, monitoring and supervision of the regulated activities, price formulation and consumer protection by providing information to the general public. These activities are clearly separable from other areas of utility service management, which are controlled by competition rules.

Anti-monopoly regulations focus on other aspects of market behavior, like limitation of competition, unfair market actions, and the inappropriate price setting of companies in monopolistic position. Market regulations also deal with other areas of competition, like procurement rules and procedures. In the studied countries, organizations of supervising public procurement have already been established: for example in Hungary the Public Procurement Council under the Parliament; and in Latvia the Purchase Supervision Bureau, reporting to the Ministry of Finance.

Organization of the regulatory framework follows various patterns in the studied countries. Models are different in three aspects: (i) whether the regulatory organization is established at national level, or it is managed locally; (ii) how independent it is from the government (state administration) and consequently from politics; (iii) scope of services covered by the regulatory agency (single sector or comprehensive, covering several ones).

In most of the cases, the existing regulatory organizations were set up at central level of government. As they deal with issues affecting the entire country, their competencies cannot be easily decentralized. Examples of these nationwide regulatory agencies are from the energy sector: Sate Energy Inspection (Slovakia), Energy Regulatory Office (Poland), National Electricity and Heat Regulatory Authority (Romania), Hungarian Energy Office, Energy Regulation Council (Latvia). They are such well established organizations, that even a regional association of energy regulators has been recently created.[17]

Tasks and competencies of these energy regulators are highly differentiated. Obviously all of them issue licenses and monitor compliance, but some of them operate as sectoral ministries: they determine production limits (Albania, Estonia), set financial and performance indicators (Bulgaria, Estonia, Romania), supervise foreign trade (Estonia, Romania)[18].

However, there are examples of locally managed regulatory organizations. In Hungary, the smaller district heating suppliers are licensed and controlled by the local governments. This covers 30% of heat production and it is managed by 102 city administrations[19]. The rest of licenses were issued by the central agency (14 major power plants). This assignment of regulatory competencies is a typical characteristic of the Hungarian decentralization: shared functions and mandates reflect the two levels of the local governments' joint responsibilities.

Another interesting decentralization experiment is under implementation in Latvia. According to the approved legislation (Act on Public Service Regulators), after the local elections, starting from September, 2001 local regulators will be appointed by the local governments. The concept of this legislation is that regulators work as 'mediators' between the public authorities, consumers and service producers (suppliers). Their mandate is licensing and supervision, approval of tariffs, dispute resolution and facilitation of competition.

These new organizations will deal only with local public utility services: communal waste management, water supply and management of sewage, and heating supply under local government authorization (without co-generated electricity). Other public services remain under the control of the national regulatory agencies (power generation, telecommunication, railway, et cetera).

This new legislation was designed after four years of discussion and it fits into the general trend of separating national and local government functions. With the appointment of municipal service regulators, the need for regional state organization bodies will be lower. Within the specific Latvian environment there are high hopes that new local regulators will support privatization and competition. They might facilitate the transformation of municipal enterprises to commercial entities, they would encourage local governments to issue a guarantee for borrowing by companies, and as non-elected regulators they are supposed to represent the service rationality and promote competition.

However, municipal regulators will be appointed for four years by local governments, so their political independence is questionable. Each local council will nominate one regulator with two deputies. Administrative costs of the decentralized regulatory organizations will be financed by a regulatory fee. It is collected by local governments from the service organizations, which have to pay less then 0.2% of their turnover. This form of financing raises another problem: initial estimates show that several municipalities have to cooperate for financing a properly paid, staffed regulator. This will require good cooperation from municipalities during the nomination process, or the professional quality and capacity of local regulators will be lower.

This might increase the local political influence, when the broad expectations cannot be fulfilled. Separation of responsibilities in service provision and service production is less feasible, whilst the possibility of informal or political influence will not decrease. There are also some issues not regulated by the present legislation, like the salary of local regulators, which might be high, and the ban on future employment by service organizations. Despite these minor problems, perhaps this decentralized and comprehensive regulatory model might work efficiently in the specific Latvian economic and legal environment.

In the case of national regulatory agencies, their relative independence from the actual governments is the critical issue. There is always a high pressure on regulatory agencies, because they set the methods of price calculation, and this way influence very sensitive social policy and company financing issues. They might influence the presence of international investors in the regulated sector, which is also a sensitive political issue. National governments tend to keep the critical elements of regulation or they directly control these agencies through the ministerial system. Ministry of Energy (Slovakia), Ministry of Economic Affairs (Hungary) or other government units deal with the regulatory agencies.

The last question of the regulatory organizational setting is how many sectors or services are controlled by them. Previous examples show that the energy sector is the only one, where regulatory organizations are widely established. However, there are efforts to introduce similar organizational forms in other countries. In Poland, under the Office of Housing and Urban Development, a board was set up for designing regulation on water and wastewater services. Within the framework of a major international technical assistance program, all the representatives of the relevant actors (ministries, anti-monopoly office, local government association, chamber of water companies, association of sanitary engineers) participated in the work of setting basic standards. Based on analytical work, these standards were publicly discussed and the results were built into the national legislation.

6. INFLUENCE OF THE EUROPEAN UNION

There are two external incentives for the development of utility and communal provision of services in CEE. One is the perspective of enlargement of the European Union. The second is pressure from Western investors. These two are not independent from each other, but their manifestations are different. The international political integration is first discussed in this section. EU legislation refers to public utility services only in a specialized manner. Communal services are under the general competition rules, notwithstanding environmental ones. In addition, policy on services of general interest derives from cases of the Court of Justice.

6.1 General Rules

One of the most important areas of rules on competition refers to state aid. According to Article 92 of the Treaty of Rome, any aid granted by a Member State which distorts competition by favoring certain undertakings or production of goods is incompatible with the common market. The article enumerates exclusive circumstances, for example, when aid is allowed to be compatible with the common market. Local government aid that is relevant in communal services, is also interpreted as state subvention.

Equal criteria for competition is guaranteed by the definition of aid and restriction of it in particular circumstances. According to the main rule, cumulative aid is to be avoided. This principle looks like a restriction on decentralization because of the limitation of its possible influence, but it really means that decentralization cannot mean a strong local part of a large powerful state. Decentralization should be closely linked to a decrease of bureaucratic roles. From this point of view, the decentralization principle also refers to the social context of the public sector.

Urban services are influenced as a part of utility services in general. 'Public undertakings' consist of telecommunication, post, transportation, and energy supply. From our point of view the last one is the most important, because urban public utility services are closely linked to provision of energy.

According to Article 90 of the Treaty of Rome, public undertakings and undertakings to which Member States grant special or exclusive rights—which entrusted with the operation of services of general economic interest or having the character of a revenue-producing monopoly—shall be subject to the general rules contained in the Treaty. It means, first of all, the rules on competition.

Different consequences derive from this obligation. In the field of public utilities, the development of competition is necessary. It means not only breaking monopolies with ex post measurements but also adopting a specific regulatory and institutional background in the public sector.

Development of competition and regulation is needed at the same time. State regulation includes monopoly supervision and consumer protection as its most important elements.

Debate on services of general interest within the EU shows that there are efforts to put short term social considerations above the long term economic interest. There are plans to design "ways of ensuring predictability and increased legal certainty in the application of competition rules relating to services of general interest."[20] According to this line of planned EU regulations, state aid might be acceptable, as it does not distort competition, but only offsets the burdens imposed by specific obligations on these undertakings and it is essential for equality in competition.

6.2 Specific Rules

Specific ruling issues consist of legal regulation on particular utility sectors and relevant cases of the Court of Justice. As far as directives referring on public utilities are concerned, electricity (Directive 96/92/EC on electricity) and gas (Directive 98/30/EC on gas industries) should be pointed out which have been implemented at national levels by most of the Member States. These particular regulations represent a model at the same time. More important selected issues are as follows:

a) *Open access to networks:* From the point of view of the content of regulation, the most important aspect is to identify monopoly elements and the sphere of competition. In the field of public services it means, first of all, that utility networks are monopoly elements, the owning of which may restrict competition in the direct provision of services. In order to break monopolies, access to networks is to be guaranteed for any providers.

Third party access (TPA) is good from the point of local governments and consumers as clients, i.e. buyers of public services. They encounter market-based circumstances in different fields of public service provision.

b) *Separation of different functions of the state:* Mainly the position of the owner and the regulatory function should be distinguished. In the latter case, the authoritative character is necessary to be independent from the interests as an owner. This separation is important at different levels of the state, like in local governments. Known public functions like pricing, supervision, and so on, of the public sector are subordinated to these types of expectations.

The establishment of independent regulatory authorities as discussed above is grounded on this demand. Although this creation is not prescribed, the majority of the Member States adopted and implemented instructions of Directives in this way.

c) '*Unbundling*': Separation is also important on the provider-side, in order to split the possible competitive part of natural monopoly services. For this purpose, the transmission system operator should be divided from the supply system. The minimum requirement is the 'unbundling' of management and accounts of transmission grid operation and supply business. At the same time, any information limits are also important to maintain, in order to guarantee the ground of competition for providers. Many of the Member States opened up their market more widely than it was required.

TPA, separation of state functions and unbundling are conditioned by each other. Together serve the liberalization of the energy market, restricting monopolies and division of market with national borders. Anti trust legislation is strengthened further by legal principles [Kende–Szűcs, 2000: 551–586] postulated by the Court of Justice.

d) *Restriction of cross-financing:* Cross-financing limits competition is allowed only when non-competitive activities are (like supply of remote places) financed supplementary from the profit of competitive activities. However, it is prohibited if one commercially opened area is subsidized from another one, or from a non-commercial activity. This principle is linked to the limitation of aids granted by states, mentioned above, adopted for utility services, in the case in which cross-financing is regular because of the specific character of delivery.

e) *'Creaming-off':* Taking unfair advantage of profit, or 'creaming-off', is prohibited according to the main rule. It must not make an attempt to limit competition only to profitable activities, leaving only the loss from particular areas for other providers. It refers also to the case in which only most profitable activities are selected. However, through delivering supplementary (extra) services, a provider cannot be condemned.

f) *Proportionality:* A minimal limitation of competition is accepted, which is sufficient for getting closer to the particular accepted policy preferences. It is good to avoid too wide an influence. This principle derives from the Treaty of Rome as a fundamental document of the EC.

There are also other regulations of the EU, but these refer to the quality of services. These are not necessary to detail here, only main groups of them should be mentioned, for example:

- service performance standards (electricity, gas supply, etc.);
- environmental legislation (e.g. on water, waste management).

7. IMPACT OF INVESTORS

The high need for external sources in the local public utility sector has attracted various types of investments and funds. During the past decade, CEE countries were targets of numerous donor and international aid programs. These programs have not only provided funds for new investments in the region, but they have also influenced the operation and management practices.

Some of the programs had specific objectives to support institutional development in the local public utility sector. The first structural adjustment loans, which were combined with development projects and several waves of technical assistance projects of international and bilateral donor programs, have all focused on different aspects of service delivery. These programs transferred not only new technical standards and modern technologies, but they have also started to introduce a new organizational and administrative framework for market based service delivery system.

Preferred topics of these programs supported the introduction of business-like operation include: cost center based management information systems; design of capital investment financing schemes; tariff setting methods and adjustment techniques of user charges; tendering and contracting practices; regulatory mechanisms; public information systems; code of ethics in municipal decision making; and so on. These new rules had to be disseminated both at the newly created service organizations, and at different levels of government.

Central administration and legislators had to develop a new legal, regulatory and fiscal transfer system in a decentralized sector, without having proper information on the permanently changing public utility services. At local government level, the elements of a new client-contractor relationship had to be developed: service specification, performance indicators, competition, contracting and monitoring rules, details of corporate finances, and social policy consequences of service decisions all had to be learned and adjusted to the standard rules and procedures of municipalities.

External funds were provided in forms of grants and loans. International programs provided grants for environmental and regional development projects, as local public utility services are parts of the two broad program areas. Technology transfer was usually combined with some form of borrowing. By the end of the 1990s, the economy in some of the CEE countries had improved, and so the loans from the large international finance organizations were slowly changed with the credits from the more flexible commercial bank. Despite the huge efforts to develop a municipal bond issue in the CEE region, only large, mostly capital cities used this form of financing in a few cases.

All these actions have not significantly changed the financial setting of local public utility services. In more decentralized countries, national and local governments involve a more extensively private sector in the service delivery, but a competitive subnational finance market has not been developed[21]. Local government borrowing in many countries requires sovereign guarantee, which deteriorates municipal innovations and activities. The market for municipal securities is not favorable and the banking and taxation environment is not supportive.

However, those countries, which have mostly benefited from these transfers and loan programs, have learned the new 'rules of the game' during the past decade. Especially in the European Union, the needs of accession countries for capital investments are declared in relation to EU standards. As environmental protection is a key area among the conditions of EU accession, grants, loans and domestic funds are jointly planned for financing capital investments.

There are various estimates on the costs of EU accession in the environmental sectors (see Table 1.8). In three countries of our research, international studies have planned the short and long term capital investments needs for meeting the EU standards. These figures range from EUR 11 Billion (Hungary), EUR 15 Billion (Romania) to USD 42 Billion (Poland). Priorities in the first round of accession countries are the water and wastewater sector, while in Romania it is the heating supply.

Table 1.8
Costs of EU Accession
Capital Investment Needs in Infrastructure Development[23]

HUNGARY	
National Environmental Protection program (1998–2002)	
EUR 11–13 Billion	
Annually 1.7% of GDP should be used directly for environmental protection purposes	
National Program for the adaptation of the acquis (1999–2001)	
Water quality:	EUR 825 Million
Improving the quality of drinking water:	EUR 107 Million
Municipal solid waste management:	EUR 180 Million

POLAND	
Capital expenditures required for meeting EU standards in environmental protection:	
Total:	USD 22–42 Billion
Of which: water, wastewater:	USD 10–17 Billion
solid waste disposal:	USD 3–4 Billion

ROMANIA	
Capital expenditures required for meeting EU standards (short and long term needs):	
Water supply:	EUR 1.5–3.5 Billion
Sewage systems:	EUR 0.9-2.0 Billion
Wastewater treatment:	EUR 1.9–4.6 Billion
Heat supply:	USD 6 Billion
Sanitation, urban environmental protection:	USD 2.5 Billion
Communal services (street, park maintenance):	USD 1.3 Billion
Public lighting:	USD 0.9 Billion

This rather high demand for investments cannot be financed from one single source. Domestic and international funds, both in forms of grants and loans should be made available. (Estimates on Hungary show that by the year of targeted EU accession, local governments have to invest

3% of GDP and in addition local public utility companies investments will be 3.2% of GDP[22]. According to these estimates, they will be mostly financed by loans, especially at the company level (2% of GDP), but at local governments it is still 0.5% of GDP).

Assuming that a similar trend will be followed by the other first and second round accession countries, new local public utility service organizational and management methods have to be developed. Donors, professional investors and especially financial institutions require modern mechanisms of service delivery, which are adjusted to the market. Otherwise cost recovery, profitability or repayment of loans cannot be expected. This pressure from investors will have a significant impact both on local public utility sector and local government finances.

In some of the studied countries basic changes are needed for having access to capital markets. In Romania, local governments should be allowed to hold accounts at commercial banks, instead of the presently authorized National Bank of Romania; assessment norms of local governments' credit risks should be made different from other commercial entities, because municipalities have a more stable revenue flow.

Rigid administrative structures might also limit local government and service company borrowing capacity. In most of the EU accession countries, regionalization is required for planning and programming purposes, but transforming the regions to administrative units will have an adverse affect: central allocation of funds and establishment of artificial service areas will create inefficient units. Hungarian and Latvian examples show that administrative regions might hinder spontaneous cooperation among local governments or service organizations. Irrational catchment areas of services, and inefficient service organizations do not support inward investment, or the inflow of funds for public utilities.

Autonomy in local government property management is also a basic condition for attracting external funds. In Romania, where the county ('judet') level service organizations dominate the public utility sector, municipalities should be encouraged to cooperate in service delivery. As regional services are controlled by the county councils, other local governments cannot invest in joint-stock companies. This will not make the municipalities as users of these services interested in management and finances of local public utility services.

Limitations on local government borrowing are also important factors of local public utility financing. The European Union criteria on public debt (60% of GDP) and public budget deficit (3% of GDP) are also used for local government budgets, as they are parts of the general government expenditures. These requirements have initiated the introduction of local government borrowing limitations even in the most decentralized countries.

In Latvia, where local governments finances are rather dependent on national transfers a special borrowing council issues the permits on municipal loan projects. There are approximately 100 local applications for loans and to issue guarantees for local borrower. The total amount of increase in local government liability is set by the annual budget (e.g. it was LAT 21 Million, 85% loans). The loans are mostly used for infrastructure (43%) and power (24%) sector investments. The guarantees are issued primarily for the district heating (44%) and water (26%) sector.

The Ministry of Finance makes the detailed assessment of the loan requests both from technical and financial point of view. As a basic rule 20% of local own and shared sources should cover the principal and interest payments. The borrowing council may recommend the use of a different bank than it is indicated in the request, if more favorable conditions are achievable.

In the decentralized local government system of Hungary and Poland, indirect rules are set for limitations on municipal borrowing. In both cases, the scale of municipal borrowing is connected to local government revenues. Municipal debt service (including guarantees) cannot exceed 70% of own source revenues in Hungary; 15% of total local revenues in Poland. The Polish legislation is more sophisticated, because the limit is further decreased if the total public debt is getting closer to the EU criteria (60% of GDP), by declining the limit to 12% of revenues, when the debt is at 55% and prohibition of municipal borrowing, when it reaches the 60% threshold. For developing an efficient capital finance market at a local level, the role of the national government should be regulated as well. It is partly the interest of the international lenders and other investors to clarify how can the national budget intervene in municipal finances. It is especially important to regulate the local bankruptcy procedures. When conditions of national budget bail-out are set, it will encourage local government borrowing.

Example of the Hungarian legislation shows, that procedures set by the law on local debt adjustment have prevented municipal bankruptcies and increased the chances of liable council decisions. The concept of municipal bankruptcy regulations focuses on procedures to be followed in case of unpaid debt by setting deadlines, defining minimum service requirements, order of payments and gradually limiting the competencies of elected bodies.

Both loan limits and legislation on bankruptcy procedures support responsible local government capital investment decisions. In some cases these regulations were initiated by international technical assistance programs and favorably influenced the inflow of external investments and creation of stable capital markets. They are important factors for developing the local public utility services.

A similarly high emphasis was put on price setting mechanisms in local public utilities. It was a relatively new practice in the CEE countries to finance local public utilities mostly through user charges. It required strong political commitments from the decision makers; accounting practices should have provided the relevant information for cost allocation; local (municipal or company) revenue administration should be developed to support user charge based service financing; welfare system should be capable to deal with the new problems; whilst methods of price setting and techniques of price increasing formulae should be widely known.

All these conditions were developed slowly during a learning process. It was in the investors' and companies' interest to widely advertise and disseminate these models and methods of price setting. Following the first decision on the assignment of price setting authorities, the other conditions of user charge based financing systems were established differently in particular sectors.

Those services were preferred, where metering was feasible: water and waste water management, and municipal solid waste deposition. Other services like district heating, rents, and solid waste collection were more based on indirect measures of consumption. Countries with high social housing stock (e.g. Latvia, Poland, Romania) are especially faced with the technical problems of allocation of service costs. In large housing estates, individual metering and regulation of service consumption is complicated and costly. This makes the market based solutions of public utility financing less attractive and less manageable.

Professional investors in local public utility sector intend to develop public-private partnership arrangements. Concessions were regulated in the early stages of transition, but local utility services were not always part of this legislation. Practices of managing build-operate-transfer schemes are also slowly developed. Lack of responsive banking services, professional and management capacity both at local governments and service organizations, along with revenue instability are the main obstacles of complex forms of partnerships.

Finally, the efforts for transforming the energy sector had an impact on local public utility services, as well. Local public utility services are closely connected to the energy sector. They provide models for decisions affecting local governments and they have an impact on municipal services.

The energy services influence municipal utilities in several ways. First of all electric and gas supply are both strategic services, which are in the focus of privatization and the competition regulations in countries of transition. Some of the local public utilities have similar characteristics to these services (limited number of producers/generators, large transmission and distribution networks, capital intensive services, etc.), so the models developed in the energy sector might be examples or basis of changes of local services.

Most of the international examples of regulation and competition rules are based on the principles developed in the energy sector (and partially in the telecommunication). International patterns and regulations are quite clear: monopolistic position should be avoided by vertical separation of the services (production/generation, transmission and distribution) and by providing third party access to networks. This is mostly regulated third party access and not a negotiated one. These principles have to be followed in the area of local public utility services.

Secondly, local public utilities are either part of the energy sector (e.g. district heating) or they are large users of electric energy. Consequently they are heavily dependent on the rules followed by the energy sector. Mostly on the organizational forms of generation and transmission, procedures of energy price setting, defining subsidies, decentralization of distribution network.

In summary, it may be concluded, that investors have had a strong indirect impact on the development of municipal public utility sector. They have initiated those techniques and conditions of pubic utility management which are useful for efficient and modern services. Besides the introduction of new technology and transfer of know-how, investors had influenced the legislation and municipal practices. The investors' impact through international organizations and donor programs helped to increase the general level of expertise and also brought additional capital in the form of grants

8.   TRANSFORMATION FAILURES

There are not only incentives for transformation, as were mentioned in previous sections, but also heavy barriers. Conflicts derive from recent changes, so sustainability of the present results of development become questionable.

According to Figure 1.1 (section 2.), an imagined linear development was outlined. It was simplified in order to make the explanation and analysis more understandable. In reality, different stages cannot be separated so clearly, they are mixed together. For instance privatization as asset sale was going on from many respects without achieving progress in procurement or contracting. There are advantages and disadvantages of this situation. On one hand, the so-called 'spontaneous' privatization in that period, when rules and procedures were not developed, was built on the logic of searching for new owners. On the other hand, very often unfavorable agreements were made between public and private actors. Liberalized markets and regulatory environment are as yet underdeveloped. Due to it being almost impossible to expect an entirely conscious institutional development, these conflicts can be seen as natural consequences of transformation. However, the general public is not so forgiving in these situations. In Table 1.9, those elements of transformation are added, which were accumulated in this process.

As Table 1.9 shows, examining the details of transformation, and adding results to the model of gradual development, some parallel phenomena emerge. At the first stage early privatization is highlighted, which might be more conflicting in the case of natural monopolies, mixed goods and services, than for the large scale privatization in general. At the second stage, guarantees were missing partially in public procurement, other tendering process, contracting out practices. Due to various reasons, transformation has been postponed in some sectors.

This accumulation of transformation effects leads to six phenomena, at least, will be discussed here:

i)   transformation to private monopolies;

ii)   corruption;

iii)   counter-interest in further changes;

iv)   social policy implications;

v)   problems of small local governments.

Table 1.9
Basic Failures of Transformation Process

	Public Utilities (natural monopolies)		Communal services (mixed goods and services)	
	Objectives	Conflicts	Objectives	Conflicts
First stage (Re-structuring)	• modest breakup of state-owned monopolies (devolution of assets) • modest unbundling • establishment of independent regulatory authority	• privatization neglecting real liberalization • creating new monopolies • strong bargaining position of service organizations • under-developed regulatory institutions	• rationalization • establishment of competitive environment	• early privatization
Second stage (Privatization)	• privatization of competitive assets • development of regulatory function • liberalization	• postponing transformation in particular sectors • moderate public procurement	• de-monopo-lization • management of public shares • privatization	• non-formalized contracting • under-controlled tendering

8.1 Emergence of Private Monopolies

When conditions of guarantees are missing, there is a real danger that state-owned monopolies are transferred to new private monopolies.[24] After the large national and international investors had gained positions in a relatively early stage of transition, they were interested in postponing full liberalization. It was made possible, because their market position became dominant, before building up a perfect regulatory mechanism. This situation is typical mainly in the utility sector.

Liberalization is more complicated than previously expected. Present monopolies are more interested in preserving existing conditions, than supporting the opening of the market to new entries. In addition, liberalization here is not necessarily equal to decreasing prices and more effective service provision.[25] Due to the collapse of the former regime, artificial low prices of energy can no longer be maintained. That is why arguing the position of monopolies is quite strong in price negotiations. It might be uncontrolled depending on the power and position of the interested municipalities.

8.2 Lack of Transparency

After the long decades of lacking almost any institutions and procedures which would ensure the transparency of public decisions, this is the most important task for the governments in the studied countries. Corruption, political or business influence in the public sector are widespread. These phenomena are caused partly by the fact that the whole transformation process was poorly planned. Perhaps this unfavorable direction of development could not have been avoided.

Problems arose from the first instance, when the privatization process itself was not designed and managed in a transparent way. This was nothing to do with the applied model or method of privatization, but rather the lack of public information, and professional and public control over the techniques of demolishing state ownership were the reasons of subsequent scandals and failures.

The more recent type of corruption derives from new possibilities. Tendering and procurement procedures are announced, only in order to cover the process of decision-making which was actually already completed. Under these circumstances, when guarantees and controls are missing, it is relatively easy to misuse procurement rules. In Hungary, for example, exceptional tendering procedures are used surprisingly often, whilst the criteria for selecting the best bids are fixed subjectively.

Problems of public procurement and tendering culminate in public utility and communal sectors. Although new legislation was passed recently in most of our countries meeting EU requirements, in practice quite a lot of insufficiency emerges.

8.3 Counter-incentives of Future Changes

Shortcomings are crucial in:
* the regulation of conflicts of interest;
* restricting corruption;
* missing the preparation of regulatory institution and functions;
* the decentralization of regulatory institutions.

Although the position of local governments can be highly appreciated, their regulatory function within their overall policy formulation is often very conflicting. This function is conditioned to supply in a unified way, and possibly independently from, direct influential linkages. The most conflicting problem is that politicians and practitioners are counter-interested in changes from many respects. That is why it is not expected from them to prepare and accept regulation of restriction on their own influence.

Modernization is firmly linked to the interested bodies, even when they are elected ones. This is true, of course, at the national level. According to a recent example, the chairman of the Hungarian parliamentary committee, responsible for supervising public procurement process was arrested due to bias committed by him passively in the investment tenders on sewage systems. However, the position of local governments, both small and large, are also regularly accused of illegal behavior.

Transparency is, in fact, a systemic problem, and not only a question of policing. Sustainability of the development reached so far is in danger. Without consciously built and forced implementation in specific institutions, it is difficult to imagine any other changes as important. It is not by chance that utility and communal sectors are highlighted in connection with this general issue. Among public functions, infrastructure is always one of the most frequented from the point of view of commissions to private undertakers and providers.

8.4 Social Policy Implications

Local public utility services were traditionally parts of the welfare system. Heavily subsidized prices and almost free access to services made public utilities key components of social policy. They were financed through cross-subsidies, nationally funded systems of in-kind contributions and equalization schemes. In reality, there were high differences in the level of local public utility services by regions, size of cities, by urban and rural communities and also among different groups of customers.

All these problems and inequalities became suddenly visible after the transformation process had already begun. In those sectors where the decentralization of service management and financing was widely used, social policy consequences were transferred to municipalities as well. This made the problems even more open, because often the low fiscal capacity and the scale of problems in service provision coincided (for example in large cities with high social housing stock, industrial regions and towns hit by economic decline).

The first stages of privatization and the transformation of service organizations have also increased the prices and consequently the social problems. Under the new market conditions, prices have suddenly multiplied in those countries and service areas where the national price control was withdrawn. Other mechanisms of the market based service provision caused social problems, for example the need for the termination of services, management of evictions, and adjustment of service costs to household income.

Subsequently, expenditures on local public utilities, including housing costs, were sharply increased. Broadly calculated housing maintenance costs became one-third of the average family income. This was significantly higher than the former share of housing maintenance. Behind the general trend, the social differentiation was the least manageable problem at a local level. Various factors behind impoverishment have multiplied, so unemployment, poor social housing conditions, and family problems jointly appeared with the arrears in public utility service payments. The price increase was partly caused by the abrupt decrease in government subsidies. Direct grants to services have disappeared in a relatively short period of time (for example in Slovakia heating subsidies have decreased to 5% between 1997 and 2000; in Hungary, the decentralization of water and solid waste price setting authority was automatically combined with a cut back in direct price subsidies). Obviously other components of the welfare system tried to compensate for these losses, but methods were not prepared for the new conditions, and demand was above the financial possibilities.

The transformation of public utility sector and local regulatory steps were very much influenced by social policy considerations. Decisions on privatization, contracting out and the introduction of other elements of competition was always assessed alongside two dimensions: impact on service quality, financial efficiency and the expected social consequences. Local government policy options were influenced by the national regulatory environment.

Primary factors were the scale and form of housing privatization. In those countries where the municipal social hosing stock remained important, rent policies and organizational forms of housing maintenance have disguised the social problems. Low rents were supposed to cover expenditures of some public utilities, but the real costs were put on the semi-public management companies. Consequently, ownership and management aspects were confused at the service organizations (e.g. in Latvia), which were not able to cope with these problems. In those countries, where the low price privatization led to broad private ownership of deteriorated apartments with typically low income families, the housing management and reconstruction costs were deferred. Price control mechanisms in some countries were designed for controlling the social problems. Centralized price setting techniques in district heating, water services (Latvia, Romania, Slovakia) are aimed at keeping the unified service charges at the lowest possible level. The other extreme solution in price setting is complete decentralization, where local government decisions are not regulated at all. There are models in between, like the rent control in Poland, where the annual amount of rents maximized in 3% of replacement costs.

The most visible sign of social problems is the high level of arrears in local utility services. District heating service is the most hard hit by unpaid user charges. In Hungary, the overdue debt is 12% of total user charges and 21% of households belong to this group[26]; in Poland 13% of families in municipal houses have had arrears for more than three months. Very often different types of debts are concentrated at the same households, so those who cannot afford district heating, also do not pay the rents, electricity bills, et cetera.

These most vulnerable groups cause the greatest problem for the local governments and for the service companies. The longer is the non-payment period, the higher is the chances of intensifying the problem of arrears. Local governments and service organizations are faced with financial difficulties because of the long collection period, which might create financial traps in an inflationary environment. They have to put a higher financial burden on those customers who regularly pay, because the fixed costs have to be recovered. This increases the chances of pushing more service users closer to their financial limits.

One of the last potential measures of the service organizations and local governments is to terminate services. Disconnection of utility services is technically not always feasible and might be rather costly for local governments. There are some public health regulations which are also against the termination (for example the water service). Indirect costs of eviction are also very expensive, when other forms of institutional services have to be provided (for the children, for the separated families, and so on).

As this is a relatively new area of legal regulations, the procedures are also complicated or cannot be implemented (for example there are no sub-standard flats to move non-paying families). Legal process might take several years and it does not have preventive effect. For example in Poland 5% of tenants were sued for non-payment of rent. The court decision and number of executed evictions have increased in comparison to the previous year.

Local governments also have other tools to deal with the social consequences of transformation of public utility services. The social benefits systems are still operated at a certain level. Under centralized structures (Romania, Slovakia) they are directly paid by the national budget: in Romania 40–60% of tenants receive benefits, which are set at a regressive scale to income; in Slovakia district authorities provide housing subsidies. In a more decentralized models (Hungary, Latvia, Poland), local governments are responsible for welfare payments and they are partially reimbursed or granted by the national budget.

Local autonomy is partially regulated by setting the types and forms of these benefits. Within this framework, municipalities disburse payments for those recipients who meet the local criteria. In Hungary only the types of locally provided social benefits are set (for example housing maintenance benefit), but local governments receive a general grant for all the local social benefits. In Poland, local housing benefits are connected to a nationally set income (in percentage of minimum pensions).

Means testing and targeting of benefits at a local level raises the problem of measurement and public access to information systems. Both local governments and service organizations have a more or less detailed register of citizens with social problems. In a privatized local public utility system the service companies are not authorized to transfer their information on non-payers and delayed payments to local governments, who in principle allocate benefits. This personal information cannot be merged with other databases, even if the recipients would benefit from it.

The social policy problems of transformation in service delivery should be solved within the frameworks of the privatization. In those countries where key components of service management are still controlled by the national government (price setting, service provision, etc.), there the general benefit system should deal with the social problems. In a decentralized setting, where local governments are responsible for all the technical, organizational, management and financing aspects of service delivery, they should also deal with the social issues. Assuming a national system of social insurance, general legislation on social policy measures, and through some forms of intergovernmental transfers, municipalities should be able to cope with the local social problems.

Within the national system of social policy, three actors have to develop the locally feasible and manageable solutions. Examples from the most decentralized countries show that municipalities, the service companies, and the indebted households should cooperate in developing a benefit and compensation system. They are all interested in decreasing arrears, diminishing delayed payments and reducing household debts to the minimum level. By creating common funds and designing joint policies on eligibility criteria and forms of subsidies, they would all benefit from the joint actions.

Service companies could get their uncollected charges, so the burden on average customers would decrease and the general image of the company would be improved. Local governments could target their benefit payments and might prevent the escalation of social problems. Service users will be identified more precisely and through new forms of support (e.g. counseling on household debt management) the 'debt-trap' might be avoided. It is crucial to develop preventive methods of social policy, because the accumulation of debts would make the potential solutions more expensive.

8.5 Problems of Small Local Governments

Local government systems in Central and Eastern European countries fit into two categories by the size of municipalities. The first one is the fragmented model of local governments, where the number of small size municipalities is high. The Czech Republic, Hungary, Latvia, Slovakia are the typical examples, where three-quarters of localities are below the population size 2,000. In these small towns and villages lives 20–25% of the population.

The other is the integrated model, where the lowest level of elected government consists of several geographical units. The best example is Poland, where only one-quarter of the population lives in villages with a population under 2,000. Here, the amalgamation of small municipalities and the creation of intermediary local governments was implemented (there are other integration models in the form cooperation, which will be discussed later).

Local public utilities have to be organized within this legal and administrative framework. The economic rationality of utility service provision requires large units in order to achieve optimal size of service production. In the very capital intensive service areas there are strong incentives at the service organizations to achieve economies of scale. Water service, district heating, solid waste deposition are the best examples of these sectors. Minimum average costs are different by activities, but usually they are above the threshold of a population of 150,000, so catchment areas in the water sector and solid waste management covers several municipalities.

Economic rationality is behind the present national financial regulations. For example in Hungary, cooperation in capital investment is subsidized by a higher matching ratio in municipal grants for landfill construction. In Poland, the share of fixed costs must not exceed 30% in the price formula, setting an incentive for establishing larger service organizations with lower network related costs.

There are different solutions for matching the administrative, political and economic considerations. Integration by mandatory amalgamation and assignment of regional service competencies to intermediary level of government are typical solutions. In Romania and Slovakia, the regional governments/administrative offices are responsible for these services. In Latvia, those local governments which do not have the service facilities are obliged to cooperate with other local governments, assigned by Cabinet of Minister's decision. In this case mutual payments are also defined. These compulsory forms of cooperation are mostly used in education and social care.

The other option is the voluntary cooperation, encouraged by legal and financial incentives. Countries with fragmented municipal structures have developed various structures and forms for joint service delivery. Legal forms of cooperation might be different by type of services or closeness and legal binding character of localities. Almost half of municipalities participate in some forms of cooperation. For communal services local governments usually operate joint institutional associations. In Latvia, co-operation agreements are signed and based on this, and local governments establish common service institutions or common enterprises. In Slovakia, municipal associations are used for joint service delivery. Under this scheme, local shares and financial sources are put together and associations have their own name, statutes, accounts, decision making bodies, et cetera.

Occurrence of cooperation forms in local public utilities depends on the scale of privatization. In Latvia, the joint provision of public services is most frequent in solid waste management (26% of surveyed municipalities), public transport (23%) and communal services (14%), unlike Hungary, where only 2% of joint forms of cooperation are in the communal sector. Here, the private provision of services is more typical, so integration is implemented through the market, when service companies establish contractual relationship with several small municipalities.

Market mechanisms always play integrative roles in local public service delivery. Even if service companies are owned by several municipalities, the smaller shares of individual municipalities does not give enough strength to control the company's business decisions and expansion strategy. Sometimes the dominating share holder (e.g. central cities) has decisive power in these joint companies, which puts the smaller ones into a losing position. Only the competition rules and contracting procedures are able to protect the interest of the smaller companies in the private sector based service system.

9. POLICY FORMULATION PROCESS

Local public utilities are formed in a very complex policy environment. First of all several components of the legislation have impact on them. Sectoral laws set the basic technical regulations: organizational and management practices are influenced by the public administration structure, commercial law and related tax regulations; rules on financial competition, consumer protection, public procurement, and so on.

Within this legal framework, policy formulation is influenced by multi-level governments. International conventions, laws and especially the European Union directives set targets for the national and local legislation. There are also various actors who might be involved in the legislative and policy making process. Regulatory agencies, local government associations, representatives of the professional and business community, and consumer protection agencies are all involved in the policy formulation, in addition to the traditional political and government institutions.

That is one reason why often such a long time is needed for approving sectoral laws. It took two years to approve the water service act in Poland, the solid waste management law was approved after five years of debate in Hungary. After the agreement on the scope and approach of these basic acts, the adjustment to changing conditions will be faster.

Following the vertical dimension of policy making in the CEE countries, the European Union is the highest source of influence. Directives are built into national laws of the accession countries through the negotiation process, often with some derogations in the law harmonization. EU legislation is highly respected even in the second round accession countries, because of the grant system combined with the policy influence.

At the level of national parliaments, the political mechanisms influence the policy making process. This institutional setting is not very stable in the CEE countries. During the past decade, leading parliamentary forces were always changing after national elections, the typical coalition governments also made an additional twist in policy making. These conditions caused unexpected changes in the conditions of local public utility services, like the privatization policy, institutional system of regional development, and so on.

In the same way that public utility services are regulated by numerous pieces of legislation and government policies, the ministerial structure is also fragmented. Usually there is no one central government agency which would be able to represent even a group of utility services. Above the traditional acts, for example the environmental protection law, regional development system, fiscal planning rules, regulations on non-profit organizations are all new strong components in the policy making process. The sectoral ministries also have to learn new roles in this fragmented and decentralized policy environment, after they have lost their state ownership based on a direct means of influence.

The national level decision making process is made even more complex by creating new institutions. In some sectors (mostly in the energy sector), regulatory agencies were created with some limited autonomy. There are organizations for controlling the competition and public procurement process. Consumer protection is often still centralized in these countries. Law enforcement is a critical condition for the efficient operation of these agencies, which made the role of the court system even more important. Professional, impartial and quick legal decisions are critical for the policy formulation.

National policy making is influenced by other than political, juridical and government institutions. The three-party-negotiations between employers, governments and unions are critical in the labor intensive sectors, which provide services critical for the economy.

Local government associations are also heavily involved in the decision making, especially in those countries where they are unified (for example in Latvia and Slovakia). Here they function like national agencies, representing the multi-purpose local governments. In Latvia, the local government association representative participates at the weekly meetings of state-secretaries, and has a consultative right at the cabinet meetings. In countries with several competing local government associations, they are involved only in the legislative process by giving opinion on laws, annual budget, and other such matters.

In the decentralized and privatized system, professional associations of service organizations were established rather quickly. They are mostly organized by sectors or by other criteria (for example in region and size), and the cooperation is effective. They initiate changes in legislation and sometimes are able to take over some of the regulatory functions of the ministries as well. This potential of water, solid waste, and public transport company associations has not, as yet, been utilized properly in the studied countries.

This long process of policy formulation, affected by several actors and changing techniques is implemented when basic goals go through a transformation. A shift from efficiency goals to equity objectives made the assessment of policies even harder. The efficiency of local public utilities and communal services is not easily measurable. The performance measurement and cost allocation problems were expanded by the special conditions of transition.

Lack of information hampered sound policy design in local public utilities. In general, data is not available on local utility and communal service organizations. In those countries which went through the transformation process, the traditional forms of information collection and registration do not work. The sectoral ministries information basis is linked to the system of subsidies (if it exists), the ministries, department responsible for local governments have to rely on indirect data sources (local government property register, Central Statistical Office data on service performance and management).

New information sources are still under development: register of incorporated entities, chamber of commerce or professional associations of service organizations might also provide data on these sectors. However, they are never complete and comprehensive: the company register involves data only on potential activities; associations do not cover all the service entities. The most reliable data is based on surveys prepared for various purposes, for example for donor programs, like our research (for example in Latvia).

Information on the organizational forms of service providers is even less reliable. Only surveys are used for testing the ownership form, output, and efficiency of these service organizations. They focus mostly on the cities and urban areas, village and sub-regional entities are not properly represented in the analyzed countries.

Lack of information was not only problematic for our comparative research. It is a major obstacle for policy design in the relevant ministries and other actors of policy making (local government and professional associations, parliamentary committees, customer protection groups, and so on). The argument for any modification of legislation, or changes in regulations is based on incomplete data, using examples of extreme cases or averages, hiding the variations by type of local government.

Incomplete picture of these sectors does not help to develop competition rules (who is the subject of competition: private or public entities); does not support the transparency and targeted character of the national capital investment subsidies.

The problems of measurement and lack of information are not the only obstacles of policy design. The time elapsed since the transformation of these sectors is relatively short. The analysis, based on the available incomplete information cannot answer the long term trend of local utility and communal services. Short term costs in service provision might be caused by the structural changes, which will be compensated in the long run.

However, some practical lessons might be drawn from this multi-level policy making environment with several actors:

- all the actors of local public utility service provision should be involved in the policy making, otherwise the desired changes cannot be achieved;

- without creating active alliances, no significant changes can be passed through this heavily interdependent policy arena;

- forces out of parliament and traditional political institutions matter a great deal, so they might initiate and support policy changes.

10. POLICY PROPOSALS

The welfare state was built in a market environment. Later the neo-liberal theories—developed as a response to public failures—were also criticized because of their extreme economic views on the social aspects of growth, and the belief of the ineffectiveness of public intervention. These basic expectations were transferred by international organizations to transforming Central and Eastern European countries. In the framework of pre-accession to EU, the legal harmonization involves many of the systemic elements of this model as well. Liberalization of public utility and communal sectors is one of the most important elements of the re-organization of formerly state-monopolized roles. However, the EU principles and the real practices of the member countries also sometimes diverge.

There is pressure simply to follow the model, but in reality circumstances are very different in the CEE countries. Before the neo-conservative shift in the early 1980s, market circumstances were general in all the developed countries. A decade later in the Eastern block, the first task was to transform the state socialist economy. In the developed countries, public functions did have long traditions, whilst in the Central Eastern European region, modern public functions of the state were not widespread.

That is why in this period of transformation, the primary task is not only to establish the market in the state-owned monopolized sectors, but also to develop new public functions under market circumstances. It is necessary to avoid classical market failures, arisen from natural monopolies and the production of public and mixed goods. Instead of the formerly general direct state intervention, independent public regulation should be introduced.

This task is very complicated, because state functions and assets cannot be transformed overnight. Public administration is in a contradictory position: on the one hand it is necessary to eliminate old roles remaining from the previous regime, but on the other hand new institutions are to be build.

Government (that is state) and market failures have arisen at the same time. First of all, it should be emphasized that 'state' failures are not classical government failures. They are surviving elements of the former system. Privatization and liberalization on market of particular sectors are only just emerging nowadays. However, market-orientation in sectors having already been transformed is more limited than it was expected. Market orientation policy means to diminish government failures in the public sector, and it should be the similar task in the CEE region as well.

Secondly, emerging market failures need to be faced. In those sectors which have already been privatized and liberalized successfully, market failures are necessary to be corrected by adequate institutions and other government techniques. Most of the urban services cannot be provided without any public influence. At present, market failures are very modestly limited in CEE countries. It is difficult to stop the traditional forms of state regulation and to transfer these new functions, required by the market to public regulation. Autonomy of regulatory bodies is questionable in most of the studied countries. Furthermore, public policy efforts to diminish market failures are very underdeveloped. Neither organizational structures, nor methods are built up properly.

Transformation failures therefore consist of remaining state failures and early market failures, which might strengthen each other. With more or restricted liberalization, the conflict cannot be diminished. Public sector orientation should be developed at the national and sub-national levels. A clear and complex policy formulation is needed for this field in the framework of the government program and also in local and regional development plans. The CEE region can expect less foreign capital investments in this respect, because investors are obviously mainly interested in opening the market, and they feel less responsibility for the quality of this market. A policy consistent with the Central Eastern European model of transformation should be the only possible way to avoid dangerous, populist political solutions. These policies might lead to extreme solutions, like the complete refusal of private initiatives and returning to state owned property or exclusive support of uncontrolled free market mechanisms. The strategic goal is to respond both to the challenges of state, and the newly created market failures.

In the field of local utility and communal services, progress in transforming the public functions is as important as the development of market orientation. Both of these mechanisms are dependent on each other. If transformation of the government functions was stopped before market liberalization, then the position of the state monopoly would be preserved. If privatization was implemented, but public regulation left underdeveloped, then the consumers would be threatened by unlimited power of the newly created private monopolies. Their position is further strengthened by the multinational firms, which increase their shares in the world market of public utilities. There are also chances of the worse case scenario, when unlimited public and private monopolies control production and provision of services. What is really dangerous for the new 'Wild East' is the uncontrolled private undertakings supplemented by the system of powerful, incompetent and corrupt national or local bureaucracies. In order to avoid this scenario and more exactly to diminish its existing harmful implications, a conscious and comprehensive policy formulation is required. Main elements of the proposed policies are as follows:

a) Sequence of steps in the transformation of public utilities should be designed as an integral process.

b) Developing all the critical elements of the new local public service management model.

c)   A conscious policy formulation to build—in parallel with liberalization—new public institutions and functions. First of all new regulatory functions and autonomy of regulatory institutions should be developed. Monitoring of the progress is also necessary, new institutions and procedures have to be revised regularly (e.g. public procurement rules). Changes should reach their critical mass and continuous revision has to be implemented, when it is required.

d)   Introduction of anti-corruption measures is also important on those areas which are influenced by public functions. Market segment of state orders is the least transparent field of public sector.

e)   In the legal harmonization process, European Union laws of transformation have to be preferred. But expectations of the EU are mainly liberalization criteria, in order to support the free movement of goods, services, capital and people. At the same time the transformation of public services must necessarily involve effectiveness and efficiency measures.

f)   Development of consumer protection is unavoidable. It is one of the most important guarantees, because the public is not equal to government.

g)   Finally, the policy design process on local public utility and communal services should be improved. There are various interconnected aspects of public utilities and consequently there are so many actors, that all of them should be involved in policy making, otherwise no long term solutions can be developed.

10.1   Arranging the Sequence of Steps for Creating Market Environment

Many pitfalls of transition countries can be avoided if the entire process of transformation in the public utility sector is properly planned. The first most important issue is the liberalization, which means the creation of the market environment and its support by public actors. There are quite a lot of counter-interests against liberalization in the public utility sector, because it has an impact on various state and private actors enjoying monopolistic positions.

On the other hand, modernization needs investments with guaranteed returns, by ensuring monopolistic positions, at least temporarily. Then, in an optimal case, a strengthened market starts to work in a favorable economic and social environment. Pace and sequence of implementation steps might be different, depending on sectors and countries. The market environment is emerged either at the beginning of the process, or at the end. For example, in typical cases electricity is re-organized gradually, but the water sector is liberalized in a different way.

There are various examples from countries in Central and Eastern Europe on inappropriately designed transformation processes. In several countries, the agency managing the state owned property launched widespread privatization before establishing powerful regulatory institutions.

Management buy-outs and other forms of 'privatization' were used before the conditions of property transfer and decentralization were designed. Tendering rules and procedures were not available, neglected or often misused in the early stages of transformation of the utility sector.

The general conclusion is that liberalization as a crucial stage of transformation should be put at the forefront. Otherwise monopolies are established without any control of the market. Full spontaneity of this process should be avoided. Liberalization is a key instrument in the fight against monopolization in many fields. Complex economic, regulatory, organizational and social welfare policies should be developed for the de-monopolization of utility and communal services. The policy actions discussed in the following sections are linked to one or other elements of this complex policy process.

10.2 Developing a New Model of Local Public Management

As mentioned in section 2, the main tendency in the provision of public services is the strengthening of private characteristics and to support exclusion in consumption. Some of the urban public services have already been made private. The other policy highlighted here is to prefer market instruments in the public sector: making incentives for competition; establishment of independent regulatory functions; and widening the basis of contractual relationships, and so on.

These crucial changes are in the background of changing the character of services, i.e. moving from public goods to toll goods. In the case of mixed goods, the tendency is the functional separation of different roles. At the same time, linkages between different social actors should become more formalized. Service provision in natural monopolies is also changing in this direction. Different positions are specified and separated from each other (for example, the client and provider split must be realized). The basis of functional separation is a demand to specifically localize and limit public responsibilities.

Figure 1.4
Public Service Management Relationship

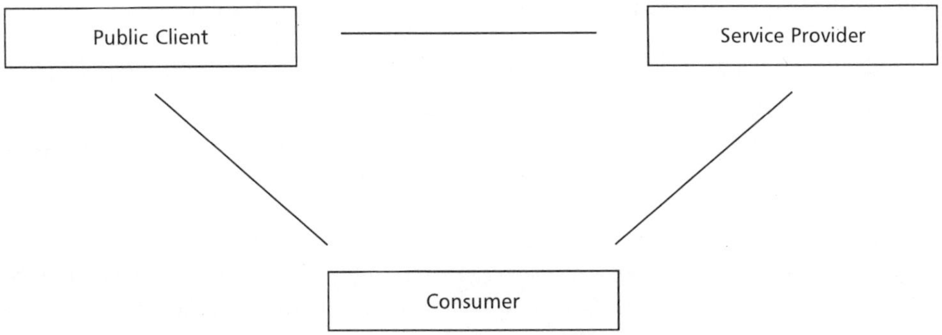

Analysts and policy-makers faced this phenomenon in the process of privatization.[27] The borderline between ownership, management responsibilities and regulation should be defined. A similar distinction should be made in connection with the provision of public services, however the starting point here is not the relationship to property, but to service.[28] The functions of the three actors should be separated: service producers, individual consumers and public clients.

The roles of the three main actors consist of the following functions:

1) *The public client's* possible roles consists of the following functions:

- client in public contracts (park and urban road maintenance, public cleaning, waste removal and disposal;

- control of service delivery (specifying services, monitoring, managing complaints, etc.);

- setting prices (depending on the regulation and the extent of privatization).

Regulation is not mentioned among the public functions, because it is more linked to the correction of market failures and less to the public management of services.

2) *The role of the public service provider* (the contractor) is:
- to deliver public services;
- to make a contract with the public clients;
- to make a contract with individual consumers;
- to participate in price setting (depending on the extent of assigned public functions).

3) *The consumer's* role includes
- to benefit from the public services received;
- to pay fees and user charges;
- to protect their interest as consumers;
- to simultaneously vote as citizens.

The last one is interesting from the point of view of public and mixed goods, because some of them are provided as mandatory services, when provision is assigned by law (e.g. maintenance of basic urban infrastructure) and they are subjects of constitutional rights (human services).

The model of direct state service provision is followed by this three pole model. A typical argument for this model of new public management is that in this way, costs can be decreased and service performance improved. In CEE countries, it has not been proved that this separation of functions actually improves the service performance, but that a decrease of costs must be true on the service providers' side. The number of employees is declining in these sectors and service performance became modestly better. Involvement of private undertakings in provision of public services was not the only possible way to decrease costs. Other options were also arisen in these countries.[29] The common provision of services can be a good chance for the municipalities with small capacities. It would be especially important in these countries, where local governments have quite limited capacities (Czech Republic, Slovakia, Hungary).[30] However, here municipalities are reluctant to cooperate with each other.

The other possible strategy is to purchase services from local governments with larger capacities. This solution is also conflicting at this stage of development, because cooperating rules are missing, and principles of compensation are not clarified. Finally, a formalized contracting out system would also be useful to guarantee clear linkages between the three parties in provision of public services.

The real question in the new model of local management of public utilities is not 'how far can we go with the market mechanisms?' Throughout this paper the conclusion is that external conditions of market mechanisms are the critical issues. Markets might create private monopolies, which should be avoided in the local utility sector by creating those regulatory environment and competition rules, which are mentioned in our paper.

Parallel to the development of market mechanisms through supply side techniques (for example 'unbundling') there are other possibilities as well. They are not discussed in our paper, but various techniques of New Public Management (NPM) are efficient responses to public failures. They are adjusted to specific conditions country by country, so emphasis of NPM is different: more competition in UK, and further private sector mechanisms (accounting, management, etc.) in Germany. Other micro level management (company, municipality) techniques are also important for improving service efficiency (for example strategic planning, technical and financial standards, and accounting practices).

10.3   Shift to Regulation

As far as regulation is concerned, more detailed codification has been missing for a decade. This lack of comprehensive legislation was due to rapid transition. First the basic conditions of service provision and efficient operation of the local public utility sectors had to be established. The sequence of institutional changes requires the second stage of transformation, which is a shift to regulatory issues.

The broad concept of regulation covers not only the classical techniques of regulatory activities, but includes competition rules and protection of public interest as well. As the examples of the studied countries showed, the regulation is very much influenced by the scale and form of privatization and the development of the legislative process. Usually, regulatory changes are started by the introduction of competition rules. The traditional institutions of consumer protection try to follow the changes in the market and to build responsive and capable organizations. The third, classical element of regulation is forgotten.

Components of the regulatory system were presented in section 6, so here only the most crucial elements will be highlighted. These are heavily discussed in all the selected countries, which try to develop a properly operating regulatory environment.

Third party access needs to manage market failures in order to avoid emerging monopolies. Developing efficient regulatory mechanisms is conditional for effective contracting mechanism. It is between equal partners that obligations can be enforced by court. CEE countries are, at present, far from achieving this stage. Now, regulation means here something more administrative and technical in this region.

As most of the local public utility services are financed by user charges to some extent, the price setting mechanisms should be developed. It is not a simple technical function, but all the related aspects of user charge based service financing should be considered. Aside from completing the tasks to design the methods of full cost pricing, a proper information basis for price formulation should also be established.

In several areas of local public utility services, benefits of user charged based service financing cannot be utilized, simply because of the lack of metering. The regulatory concept on pricing should deal with this problem, and metering should be incorporated into the proposed solutions. This requires capital investments (e.g. in district heating), changes in local government policy making (shifting from tax based financing to user charges) and improvement in revenue administration, both at local governments and at service organizations. There were numerous innovative techniques developed in particular service areas (e.g. in solid waste management).

Another similarly important condition for price regulations is the capability to deal with the social policy consequences of user charges. The economic advantages of priced based service financing can be realized only when the emerging social problems are solved at the same time. This aspect should not be neglected by the public utility policy makers, because all the three actors (client, contractor and customer) are interested in solving the social problems raised by the market. Their responsibility is common, so all of them should be involved in the financing and management of the available methods.

Another important element of the regulatory environment is to deal with the problem of the so-called 'services of general public interest'. In the European social tradition, the equal access to public services dominate the regulatory concepts. According to this approach, no limitations should be imposed on public property rights. It is especially important under the present circumstances when large, international organizations provide formerly local basic services. Tendering and contracting practices ensure efficient service delivery, but local governments may lose their traditional methods of influence.

If these mechanisms are not ensured, local governments may react negatively to this shift in controlling techniques and they may choose extreme solutions, like neglecting the entire practice of tendering. There are various attempts to deal with this problem: introduction of the 'best value' approach in the United Kingdom or to interpret the compulsory tendering rules selectively in Hungary. This is an existing problem, which should be solved in CEE countries, where regulatory concepts are still under development.

For developing efficient regulatory mechanism, the administrative capacity of national and local governments should also be improved. Following the present stage of transformation, when legal harmonization and modernization of ownership structures are the most important goals, necessary human resources should be developed as well. Without qualified staff and administrative organizations, the regulatory functions will not operate efficiently.

Technological development also influences the methods of regulations in public utilities. The horizontal integration of network based services has an impact on the planning, administration, and human resource management of companies and competencies of local governments. The example of the German urban utility companies (e.g. 'Stadtwerke') showed that a new relationship was established between the service organizations and the local governments. Opening of the markets forced municipalities to re-design their core service activities and to adjust to new ownership and management structures. Similar changes are expected in countries of Central and Eastern Europe.

Finally. the regulatory systems are still influenced by the dominant public service, the energy supply. As we saw in the studied six countries, it is a sector which determines several other local public utilities. Energy supply is important, because some local services are a part of it (e.g. district heating) or because they are heavily dependent on it (e.g. water sector). The privatization of energy might be an example for other sectors, so the regulatory mechanisms are also adaptable in other areas. It might serve also as the basis of a comprehensive regulatory organization in the future.

10.4   Improving Transparency

Corruption and biased decisions are not only problems of public service management, but they influence the whole public life in CEE countries in this phase of transformation. Typical examples are public utility and communal services, in which budget sources; public procurement; and public contracts in general are widely used. The experience is that rules of public procurement work without sufficient guarantees and continuous monitoring of the systems is almost missing.
On the other hand, although conflicts of interest are always under discussion in parliaments, passing real effective regulation is restricted in different manners. Belief in any type of 'code of ethics' for public servants is also very weak, skepticism cannot be broken down against experiences like this.

Despite of the many inefficient attempts, local policy-making should have a role in changing these processes. It would be necessary to develop mechanism for the improvement of transparency at first local and regional levels. It depends very much on political consensus, that is hard to reach in this phase of development. However, efforts should not be neglected because of the present bad experiences.

The system of public procurement has already been introduced in most of the countries in the region. However, unfortunately, introduction is not enough, continuous development is necessary, because players can learn techniques to avoid barriers which are unpleasant for them.

Openness and transparency of the price setting mechanism is also important. Political decisions can be made when selection of methods is simply enough to define priorities. On the other hand, control should be done over actions of providers.

Conflicts of interest are widespread in the region, and their problems are heavily discussed by parliaments, local councils and the general public. However, very powerful counter-interest exists both at the national and local levels. Despite of this fact that several legal rules are legislated, the main problem is that restrictions are not supported by the political behavior of various actors. More detailed legal regulations, enforcement mechanisms and rules of public behavior are needed at the same time.

10.5   Adjustment to European Union Requirements

Local policy formulation should not directly adopt any EU norms before accession. In the process of legal harmonization a lot of requirements are passed, but these obligations derive from the national legal system. In this respect, adjustment does not mean more than following basic policy expectations. There is no intention to be exhaustive in mentioning some of the more important general policy expectations which may be relevant from the point of view of public utility and communal services.

Firstly, guarantees of competition should be focused. Preparing the ground for free competition and transparency is a precondition for the transformation of the former state sector. Direct, politically motivated or outside individual influence would be necessary to restrict.

At the same time, new forms of public regulation have to be developed, from which different roles are defined for subnational governments. Guaranteeing open access to networks is favorable for local governments as clients (buyers of services). Additionally, local responsibility exists for maintaining open access in some of the service areas which are exclusively under local control.

Furthermore, mutual trust among governmental, private and non-governmental sectors in the realization of communal and utility tasks is also important. This is not only a question of free competition. A specific view is also necessary to be adopted in order not only to implement EU regulations, but to realize same aspects continuously in working policy formulation processes. Implementation has some costs as well: legal harmonization has an impact on capital investments (e.g. MSW); law harmonization is a complicated legal task for the government administration and for the legislation (see conflicting pieces of legislation is some countries); long debates over some basic laws (e.g. environmental legislation).

10.6   Consumer Protection and Social Policy Considerations

During the past decade, the development of public utility services has been influenced by different factors. In the first period, the emphasis was on the improvement of service performance, demanding capital investments, and the raising of technical standards of services. Later it was combined with financial requirements because the necessary resources should be made available. Efficient service delivery and modern financial techniques were the necessary conditions for internal and external funding. Later, the social policy aspects of utility and communal services became high priorities. But these social considerations should be balanced with technical (capital investment) goals and financial (efficiency) objectives in the development policies. In the case of local public utilities, all these three aspects of transformation should be developed jointly.

One form of ensuring social policy objectives is to establish customer protection mechanisms. This a crucial condition for developing a modern regulatory system. Independent and professionally sound regulatory institutions automatically protect the interest of the consumers. They have an impact on service performance through the licensing, and the monitoring of service delivery. They might prevent customers from a major breakdown of utility services by guaranteeing professional standards and financial disciplines at the service organizations. By controlling price setting, regulatory bodies may ensure the principles of lowest cost pricing, fair methods of price adjustment formulae, and the curbing of unjustified increase cost pressure of service organizations. This influence on price setting mechanisms is extremely important in an inflationary economic environment, which was typical in almost each of the CEE countries.

Social policy objectives are often misinterpreted in the utility sector.[31] The example of the energy sector shows that keeping prices at an artificially low level will lead not only to economic inefficiency, but to unexpected social consequences. Low energy (or any other utility prices) or lower VAT tariffs will provide more subsidies to large consumers, who are probably better off than the poor ones. This will also lead to economic distortions and import dependent sectors for high budget subsidies. The preferred status of these public service providers might also lead to monopoly situations, which further accelerates inflation. So the present practice of flat low utility prices in many CEE countries should be moved towards market based prices. This shift should be combined with targeted social policy measures, with means tested subsidies and other social policy measures.

10.7   Impact on Policy Making Process

The complexity of local public utilities and communal services requires a multi-dimensional approach in designing the future of these sectors. Legal, financial, organizational, management and social factors are equally important components of development policies. The basic principles and rules have to be changed in a relatively short period. Under these circumstances implementa-tion of any major shifts in service delivery moving from state control towards regulation cannot be built into the daily practice without changing the policy making process.

Some basic conditions of sound and professional policy formulation should be developed along the lines of an efficiently working public information system of local public utilities. There are several groups who are interested in the future of these sectors, therefore all of them should be involved in the policy making process. Despite the highly technical character of the utility and communal services, policy options and alternative solutions should be presented to all the interested parties.

It is especially important to involve those public and customer groups, who are not a part of the traditional political and administrative policy making process. Trade unions, consume protection agencies, employers' organizations, local government and professional associations all should have a say in designing the future of the local public utility sector. However, the culture and methods of transparent and professional policy formulation can be developed in the CEE countries during a long learning process.

The roles of the policy makers and politicians are usually mixed in the utility sectors. In these sectors of 'strategic' importance and with direct linkages to market, politicians and practitioners have to cooperate closely. This might lead sometimes to a confusion of roles, like in the management and supervisory boards of local utility companies, in price setting authorities or in contract awarding bodies.

REFERENCES

Ágh, Attila, *The Politics of Central Europe*, London: SAGE, 1998.

Bokros, Lajos, *A társadalmi szolidaritás és annak hiánya* (Solidarity and its deficit in the society) Budapest: Élet és Irodalom, 8 June 2001.

CEDEC, *Strategies for the Liberalized Market*, Bonn-Cologne (European Confe78deration of Public Sector Energy Distribution Companies), 2000.

Ehrlich, Éva, *International Tendencies: Infrastructure and Services in Hungary*, published in: Csáki, György ed. Transition—Infrastructure, Budapest: Institute for World Economics of the Hungarian Academy of Sciences, 1994.

ERRA 4th, *Annual Regional Energy Regulatory Conference Proceedings*, Bucharest: ERRA, 11–13 December 2000.

FDI Indicators, *Fiscal Design Across Levels of Government. Central and Eastern European Countries, Year 2000 Surveys. Summary Note*, OECD: 2001.

HDU Piac, *Verseny-Szerződés. Irányítási és pénzügyi módszerek az önkormányzati településüzemeltetésben*, Helyi Önkormányzati Know-How Program, Budapest: 'Helyi Demokrácia és Újítások Alapítvány', 1996.

Horváth, M. Tamás, *Public Finance in Political Systems*, published in: Nemec, Juraj and Wright, Glen eds. Public Finance: Theory and Practice in Central and European Transition Bratislava: NISPAcee, 1997.

Horváth, Tamás M., ed. *Decentralization: Experiments and Reforms. Local Governments in Central and Eastern Europe*, Budapest: Local Government and Public Service Reform Initiative, 2000.

Hughes, Owen E., *Public Management & Administration: An Introduction,* Houndmills: Macmillan.

Hyman, David N., *Modern Microeconomics: Analyses and Application.* Homewood: IRWIN, 1989.

Kende, Tamás and Szűcs, Tamás, *Az Európai Unió Politikái.* Budapest: Osiris Kiadó, 2000.

Kornai, János, *Tíz évvel a Röpirat angol kiadásának megjelenése után: A szerző önértékelése. Közgazdasági Szemle, XLVII. évf. szeptember.* [Keynote address presented at the Annual Bank Conference on Development Economics, The World Bank, Washington, 20 April 2000], 2000.

Kungla, Tarvo, *Fiscal Decentralization of Estonia*, Discussion Papers, No. 13. Budapest: Local Government and Public Service Reform Initiative, Open Society Institute, 1999.

Lane, Jan-Erik, The Public Sector: Concepts, Models and Approaches. London: SAGE, 1995.

Langen, Werner, *Working Document on the Communication from the Commission "Services of General Interest in Europe",* Committee on Economic and Monetary Affairs, European Parliament. 2001.

Magyar Statisztikai Zsebkönyv, *International Statistical Pocketbook.* Budapest: KSH (Central Statistical Office), 1999

Mikesell, John L., *Fiscal Administration: Analysis and Applications for the Public Sector. Pacific Grove*, Brooks/Cole: 1991.

Musgrave, Richard A. and Musgrave, Peggy B., *Public Finance in Theory and Practice*, New York: McGraw-Hill, 1989.

Nemec, Juraj, *Economic and Social Basis of Government Actions*, published in: Nemec, Juraj and Wright, Glen eds. Public Finance: Theory and Practice in Central and European Transition. Bratislava: NISPAcee, 1997.

95

Nemzetközi Statisztikai Zsebkönyv , *International Statistical Pocketbook,* Budapest: KSH (Central Statistical Office), 1999.

Oates, Wallace E., *Fiscal Federalism.* New York: Harcourt, Brace, Jovanovich, 1972.

OECD, *Application of Competition Policy to the Electricity Sector,* Paris: OCDE/GD(97)132, 1997.

OECD, Oligopoly. *Diretorate for Financial, Fiscal and Enterprise Affairs, Committee on Competition Law and Policy* DAFE/CLP(99)25, 1999.

OECD, *Competition in Local Services: Solid Waste Management. Diretorate for Financial, Fiscal and Enterprise Affairs, Committee on Competition Law and Policy.* DAFE/CLP(2000)13, 2000.

Péteri, Gábor, *Önkormányzati gazdálkodás: Új lehetőségek, gyakorlati módszerek. Csákberény,* 'Helyi demokrácia és újítások' Alapítvány, 1995.

Péteri, Gábor, *Alternative Service Delivery. In: Nemec, Juraj and Wright,* Glen eds. Public Finance: Theory and Practice in Central and European Transition. Bratislava: NISPAcee, 1997.

Péteri, Gábor—Tausz, Katalin (Editors) *Megelőzés és együttműködés. A díjhátralék probléma megoldási lehetőségei helyi szinten.* Pontes Kft., Nagykovácsi: 'Helyi önkormányzati know-how' program, 1999.

Savas, E. S., *Privatization: The Key to Better Government,* Chathman, NJ: Chatman House, 1987.

Sharp, Elaine B., *Urban Politics and Administration: From Service Delivery to Economic Development,* New York: Longman, 1990.

Smith, Andy, *'Studying multi-level governance: Examples from French translations of the structural funds'.* Public Administration, Vol. 75, No. 4, pp. 711–729, 1997.

SNDP, *An Integrated Effort for Modernizing the Subnational Government System in Hungary,* The World Bank: 1999.

Stiglitz, Joseph E., *Economics of the Public Sector,* New York: W. W. Norton & Company, 1988.

Szalai, Ákos–Ebergényi, András, *Önkormányzati közszolgáltatás: magyar módszerek, lehetőségek és esettanulmányok kézikönyv.* FDI-CEE kiadvány: 1998.

Truett, Lila J. and Truett, Dale B. *Macroeconomics.* St. Louis: Timer Mirror/Mosby College Publishing, 1987.

Voszka, Éva (2000/a) *Habár fölül a gálya,* Népszabadság, 24/07/2000.

Voszka, Éva (2000/b) *Piaci zárva tartás,* Népszabadság, 19/10/2000.

Weimer, David L. and Vining, Aidan R. *Policy Analysis: Concepts and Practice,* Englewood Cliffs: Prentice Hall, 1992.

World Bank *Maintaining Utility Services for the Poor.* Washington, DC, 2000.

World Statistics Pocketbook, New York: United Nations, 2000.

NOTES

[1]   OECD, 2000.

[2]   see Weimer and Vining, 1992: pp. 41–93.

[3]   see Truett and Truett, 1987: p.40

[4]   see Musgrave and Musgrave, 1989: pp. 41–58.

[5]   see Truett and Truett, 1987: 41.

[6]   see Hyman, 1989: 665.

[7]   see especially Mikesell, Lane, 1991, 1995: p. 24.

[8]   Sharp, 1990: p. 104.

[9]   Stiglitz, 1988: p. 72.

[10] see Savas, E. S., *Privatization: The Key to Better Government,* Chathman, NJ: Chatman House, 1987: pp. 35–7.

[11] As a summary of groups of theories see Nemec, 1997: pp. 82–88.; Hughes, 1994: pp. 97–103.

[12] Unweighted average of transition indicators for banking sector, non-banking financial institutions, competition policy, enterprise reform, corporate governance. The index is based on EBRD expert judgement, it ranges from 1 to 4. See Transition Report, 2000, EBRD.

[13] Ratio of population supplied by these services.

[14] Source: Horvath, 2000 and FDI Indicators, 2001.

[15] *"MSW management modernization through the private sector"* (manuscript of an LGI project, managed by Paul Dax, 2001 Sofia)

[16] Ehrlich, Éva, *International Tendencies: Infrastructure and Services in Hungary*, published in: Csáki, György ed. Transition—Infrastructure, Budapest: Institute for World Economics of the Hungarian Academy of Sciences, 1994: pp. 24–26.

[17] Energy Regulators Regional Association, initiated by USAID, registered in Budapest in 2001 (see: www.narucintl.org/CEE–NIS/).

[18] Series of Licenssing and Competition Related Issues Papers, Paper No. 3., presented at 4th Regional energy Regulatory Conference, 11–13 December, 2000, Bucharest.

[19] *"Report on the activities of the Hungarian Energy Office in 1999"*, www.narucintl.org/CEE-NIS/Ras/Hungary/.

[20] Working document of the Comittee on Economic and Monetary Affairs, European Parliament, 13 February, 2001.

[21] For example see the report of the SNDP program on Hungary (1999).

[22] SNDP (1999).

[23] Based on the LGPP country reports.

[24] Voszka, Voszka, Éva, *Habár fölül a gálya,* Népszabadság, Budapest: 24/07/2000, 2000/a.

[25] Voszka, Éva, *Piaci zárva tartás*, Népszabadság, Budapest: 19/10/2000, 2000/b.

[26] Péteri–Tausz (1999).

[27] Compare with Péteri, Gábor, *Alternative Service Delivery. In: Nemec, Juraj and Wright,* Glen eds. Public Finance: Theory and Practice in Central and European Transition. Bratislava: NISPAcee, 1997: pp. 395–397.

[28] Péteri, Gábor, *Önkormányzati gazdálkodás: Új lehetőségek, gyakorlati módszerek. Csákberény,* 'Helyi demokrácia és újítások' Alapítvány, 1995, pp. 31–34.

[29] Kungla, Tarvo, *Fiscal Decentralization of Estonia*, Discussion Papers, No. 13., Budapest: Local Government and Public Service Reform Initiative, Open Society Institute, 1999: p. 12.

[30] Horváth, M. Tamás, *Public Finance in Political Systems*, published in: Nemec, Juraj and Wright, Glen eds. Public Finance: Theory and Practice in Central and European Transition Bratislava: NISPAcee, 1997.

[31] See Bokros, Lajos, *A társadalmi szolidaritás és annak hiánya* (Solidarity and its deficit in the society) Budapest: Élet és Irodalom, 8 June 2001.

CHAPTER 2

Open Competition, Transparency, and Impartiality in Local Government Contracting Out of Public Services

Dr. Kenneth K. Baar

Table of Contents

Open Competition, Transparency, and Impartiality in Local Government Contracting Out of Public Services

Dr. Kenneth K. Baar

1. INTRODUCTION

The contracting out and privatization of the provision of basic public services, including the operation of district heating, water and sewer services; refuse collection; and park and road maintenance is widespread in Central and Eastern Europe (CEE) and is steadily increasing in scale. Such privatization of service provision is taking place through short term contracts, long term concession contracts, and/or the sale of public service facilities.

In CEE, local governments are even more dependent on the contracting out and privatization processes than in Western Europe. Whilst governments in Western Europe can generally obtain capital at a lower interest rate than private companies in order to upgrade their systems, in Central and Eastern Europe the reverse is true—local governments are dependent on outside capital in order to undertake capital improvements. Furthermore, local governments in the CEE are under pressure to upgrade water and sewer services in order to meet EU accession standards. Also, they are under pressure to upgrade district heating systems in order to reduce the substantial financial burdens of their provision.

How the contracting out and privatization of services is conducted will determine the future costs of these basic services, which have a significant impact on household budgets, and it will determine the future ownership and control of substantial public assets.

The purpose of this chapter is to address basic issues related to the use of competitive bidding processes, transparency, and impartiality in contracting out public services in the CEE and to present a comparative discussion of practices in the EU and other nations. This chapter examines the contracting out practices in four CEE nations (the Czech Republic, Hungary, Romania, and Slovakia) and it provides a comparison discussion of practices in Western Europe and the U.S. It is based on a combination of interviews and research and is subject to the caveats that while somewhat precise information could be obtained about legislation in the CEE, widely divergent views were presented about prevailing practices, and information on actual practices has not been collected on a systematic basis.

The issues that are covered include:

a)   The applicability of procurement laws and other provisions requiring competitive procedures for the selection of contractors;

b)   Public access to contracts and information considered in price setting proceedings. (freedom of information);

c)   Requirements of impartiality and the prevention conflicts of interest in the selection of contractors.

Each of the above may be seen as a basic prerequisite to the conduct of contracting out in a manner that best serves the interests of the public. If conflicts of interest are permitted, bidding is not really competitive. Without competitive bidding for contracts, there is no assurance that the public is obtaining the most favorable terms for the provision of its services. Without transparency, corruption is more likely and public trust in the fairness of selection process is eliminated. Furthermore, without transparency, the general public is excluded from the contracting out process. As a result, the potential benefits of independent public review, criticism, and expertise are lost.

In the past decade each of these issues has been the subject of intensive public interest and legislative reform in West Europe, as well as the countries in CEE.

While the purpose of contracting out is to increase efficiency, reduce costs and/or obtain investment resources that are not available to local governments, contracting out or privatization may result in either substantial public benefits or irreversible harm. It places governments in a role that may be even more complex than that of service provider, the role of contractor and regulator. The manner in which contracting out is undertaken is critical in obtaining beneficial results. This is especially true when long term contracting is undertaken, as is common when contracting is undertaken for the purpose of inducing private companies to upgrade public service systems. Although there is no prescription to insure that contracting out will work effectively, the process by which it is undertaken can play a critical role.

While the contracting out of public services has becoming increasingly widespread in Central and Eastern Europe, the degree of contracting out differs significantly among the nations of the region. Typically, national laws authorize the contracting out of services and govern long term concession contracts. In some nations the sale of utility infrastructure is prohibited.

In the Czech Republic, privatization has always had a high place on the public policy agenda. Commonly, the physical components of infrastructure as well as operating services have been privatized. In larger cities, public ownership of water facilities has been maintained, but service provision has been contracted out on a long-term basis. In the mid-1990s, the French government funded education programs for local governments which advocated such an approach. In smaller cities, the privatization of water infrastructure as well as service has occurred. In the case of district heating, privatization of the infrastructure as well as the service provision is common in larger cities. In Prague, water service, refuse collection and park maintenance have been contracted out to private companies. Each of the city districts has authority over these services and contracts out for them individually. However, the districts have all elected to contract with the same company. The refuse and park collection contracts are for one year. As a matter of practice, they are renewed with the same company.

Under Hungarian law, local governments are not permitted to sell the physical portions of their infrastructure. It has become standard practice for cities to create one or more municipally owned companies which are responsible for park, road maintenance, snow clearing, refuse collection, and cemetery services. In turn, some of these services are subcontracted out to private firms. Typically, park maintenance services are divided into sections of the city and subcontracted out on a section by section basis, resulting in numerous subcontractors for this service. (The typical length of such contracts is 3 to 5 years). Refuse collection services are commonly contracted out to foreign firms when significant capital investments are required in order to create new disposal sites. In such cases, 25 year contracts are common. Interviewees estimated that about 10% of all water services are contracted out to private investors. Approximately seven of the 109 municipalities that have district heating systems have entered into long term concession contracts (typically 15 to 20 years) for the operation of their services. In addition, a few municipalities have entered into lease agreements in order to upgrade their systems. Under the agreements, specified improvements by a private company becomes the property of the district heating company after making monthly payments for a fixed term, typically about ten years.

In Romania, the contracting out of services is less common than in the neighboring countries. The sale of publicly owned assets is prohibited.[1] However, concession agreements are becoming widespread. Bucharest has entered into concession contracts for the provision of water and sewer and has executed five year contracts with three different companies for refuse collection. Other cities have contracted out refuse collection and/or park maintenance.

In Slovakia, about half of all cities have contracted out waste collection. Other commonly contracted out services, which are contracted out by cities and the individual districts in Bratislava, include park maintenance and street maintenance. Typically park maintenance contracts are broken down into sub areas of the contracting jurisdiction and are short term.[2] Unlike in the neighboring countries, the state is just beginning to transfer ownership of water and district heating facilities to local governments. Bratislava has sold its district heating company to a foreign company. Komarno officials indicated that plans are under consideration to sell its district heating facility.[3]

2. LAWS REQUIRING COMPETITIVE PROCEDURES

2.1 EU Directives

The EU is conditioning accession on conformance with its public procurement standards. As a result, EU regulations are viewed by the CEE nations as the standard for required practices. The EU extensively regulates the conduct of tendering in its member states pursuant to its free competition objectives and it places a high priority on conformance with its standards. Furthermore, conformance with EU procurement standards has been a precondition to EU accession. Public procurement processes have been considered as essential tools for bringing about fair competitive processes and transparency in public contracts. In the EU, as well as in Central and East Europe, policies and practices with regards to these issues are in an evolving state and detailed discussion.

Each of the CEE nations has adopted detailed procurement legislation, largely based on EU models. In the CEE countries, EU standards operate as a *maximum as well as a minimum* for the coverage and standards of procurement laws. While requirements of competitiveness and trans-parency are critical for effective contracting out, exceptions to the such requirements are widely exploited.

In the past decade, the EU has been taking steps to expand the applicability of its procurement standards to public service contracts. In 1992, the EU adopted a directive that is applicable to public services contracts. It includes a broad definition of 'contracting authorities' as follows:

- contracting authorities shall mean the State, regional or local authorities, bodies governed by public law, or associations formed by one or more of the authorities or bodies governed by public law. Body governed by public law means any body:

- established for the specific purpose of meeting needs in the general interest, not having an industrial or commercial character, and

- having legal personality and

- *financed for the most part, by the State, or regional or local authorities, or other bodies governed by public law; or subject to management supervision by those bodies; or having an administrative, managerial or supervisory board, more than half of whose members are appointed by the State, regional or local authorities or by other bodies governed by public law.*

EC Directive 92/50/EEC, 18 June 1992

However, the services directive contains some very significant exemptions. The Directive is applicable to contracts for "pecuniary interest".[4] This clause is interpreted to mean that it is not applicable to contracts under which the payment to the service provider comes from user fees rather than from the contracting authority (for example a contract between a public agency and a private company for refuse collection, supported by user fees). In line with this concept, concession contracts have been excluded.[5] This exclusion has been subject to wide criticism.

The services directive also excludes contracts for the acquisition or rental of land or other "immovable property".[6] This section results in the exclusion of the rental or sale of utility infrastructure.

2.2 Recent EU Communications

Although concession contracts and other contracts without a "pecuniary interest" are exempt from the EU's public service directive, a recent (April 2000) Commission Interpretative Communication on concessions under Community Law sets forth the conclusion that such contracts are subject to the Treaty requirements of adherence to the principles of open competition and transparency. The Interpretative Communication notes the EC rules instituting and guaranteeing the proper operation of the Single Market, including:

• the rules prohibiting any discrimination on grounds of nationality

• the rules on the free movement of goods, freedom of establishment, freedom to provide services,[7]

It further notes that:

> The principle of equality of treatment implies in particular that all potential concessionaires know the rules in advance and that they apply to everybody in the same way. The case law of the Court {...} lays down that the principle of equality of treatment requires not only that conditions of access to an economic activity be non-discriminatory, but also that public authorities take all measures required to ensure the exercise of this activity.[8]

2.3 Public Procurement Laws in CEE Countries

Consistent with the EU directives, the CEE laws have contained significant exceptions in their coverage which result in substantial exemptions for contracted out services and/or the privatization of public services. The most notable are exemptions from procurement laws and other types of public scrutiny, including:

• government contracts for services which provide that services shall be paid for directly by citizens (rather than by the local government) and, therefore, are not for pecuniary interest;

• concession contracts;

– the transfer of stock within mixed public private companies which effectively transfer control to private companies;

– the sale or rental of physical infrastructure.

In the case of Hungary and Romania, exemptions for public service contracts from procurement requirements are counter to the broader purposes of their procurement legislation. The purposes of the Hungarian law include "{...} establishing the transparency of the use of public funds and its wide-ranging public controllability, furthermore, providing for the purity of competition in the course of public procurement,{....}"[9] The Romanian procurement law sets forth similar objectives.[10]

The Czech Republic adopted a procurement law in 1994.[11] In 2000, the coverage of the law was extended to contracting out by private monopolies and city owned companies. The law exempts contracts for the purchase of water and energy, placed by producers, carriers, and distributors.[12] In addition, as in other nations, the law has been interpreted to exclude contracts for services when the services are paid for directly by the citizens, such as refuse collection, based on a provision which states that a "public contract" is understood to be a contract for "pecuniary consideration." While city purchases are covered by the procurement law, other types of transactions, including city rentals or sales of public infrastructure are not subject to such requirements. For example, a city rental of a refuse disposal site is not controlled. Another route to privatization beyond competition and public tendering requirements has been the through the creation of a company which starts with a majority share of public ownership but then becomes mostly privately owned. Besides not being subject to the procurement law, such transfers can take place without the approval of the municipal council, because councils do not have legal control over the city representative of the company. Proposals for legislation to bring such transactions under public control have not been successful. The law contains a detailed list of the information that must be included in an assessment and evaluation report by the public procurement commission;[13] however, it only provides for access to such reports only by other bidders, who may "view" the report (as opposed to obtain a copy).[14] The manager of one local government indicated that it was common practice among local governments to select criteria for procurements so as to ensure that a particular company would win a contract.

In Hungary, as in other nations, a principle exemption is created by the limitation to services for which pecuniary consideration is paid for by the city are for solid waste services supported solely by user fees. If the service is partly paid for out user fees and partly subsidized, it is covered by the Procurement Act. Furthermore, while a contract with a private company to provide user fee funded services is exempted from the procurement law, purchase activities of that private company (e.g. the purchase of trucks by a waste disposal company pursuant to the performance of public service) are covered by the act. A separate act covers the contracting out of refuse collection and chimney services.[15] But it does not set forth standards for these tenders. In some interviews, directors of municipally owned companies indicated that the activities of their companies were not covered by the procurement legislation and that their subcontracting for public services was not subject to the procurement act. Other knowledgeable sources indicated that localities were claiming exemptions on the basis that under the Procurement Act "public service providing activity" only covers activities "*qualified by ... municipal by-law* as public service, activity provided by an institution in the public service, public utility or communal service."[16]

In the course of interviews, this author found substantially differing opinions as to the scope of the Hungarian Procurement Act and statements that the law clearly did not allow for some of the interpretations which other experts claimed were common. Further clarification and possibly simplification, which obviates the need for substantial cross-referencing to other legislation, might bring about greater uniformity of interpretation.

The EC Commission, while commenting that "Hungarian legislation on public procurement is largely compatible with EC directives in this field", noted that: "… the Hungarian legislation does not meet all the requirements of EC Directives regarding the utilities sectors (namely energy, telecommunications, water, and transport).[17] In 1998, interviewees from the Ministry of Justice and the Procurement Council indicated that plans were underway to take the steps that would be necessary to bring the Hungarian standards in conformance with the EU standards by the time of accession. However, there were differences in opinions among the interviewees as to the extent of diversion between the EU standards and Hungarian law.

Romania adopted a new procurement law in 1999.[18] However, since then, its implementation has been delayed pending the implementation of regulations. The law contains a basic statement of principles which includes: free competition; efficiency in the use of public funds; and transparency; and introducing a national regulatory agency, publicity rules for tenders, and statistical reporting requirements; which were all absent from the previous legislation.[19]

Its coverage of entities which perform government functions is broad, including the operation of fixed networks which provide service to the public in connection with the provision of drinking water, electricity, gas, or heating. However, it contains an exemption for contracts where consideration consists of the right to exploit. As in the other nations, privatization can be accomplished through the creation of joint ventures without meeting public procurement requirements.

Slovakia adopted a new Public Procurement Act in 1999.[20] Concession contracts for the administration and control of physical assets of public services are now exempt.[21]

Exemptions from public procurement requirements for concession contracts and other types of public service contracts make little sense from a public policy perspective. The concept that there should be an exemption or a less stringent procurement rule because the payment for a public service comes directly from the private users rather than with public funds or that the service goes directly from the private company to the user exalts form over substance. Funds for all services come from taxes or fees paid by private individuals. Furthermore, in the case of a public service performed by a private contractor, the contractor has received a monopoly position, which has economic value, from the public sector. In light of the fact that the monopoly position has economic value, it is certainly a form of consideration. At the same time, the interests of the public in securing the benefits of the Procurement Act are the same whether the service and/or the payment for the public service is directly from the citizen to the service provider or via a government agency.

3. PUBLIC ACCESS TO PUBLIC CONTRACTS (TRANSPARENCY)

In several of the nations in the CEE region, it is common or standard practice for government agencies to take the position that contracts for public services are secret. Such secrecy has frequently become a major political issue, as result of discontent over public contracts.

Freedom of information is a relatively new right among the basic freedoms. Almost all of the nations in Europe have adopted a freedom of information law. However, nearly, all of these laws contain an exception for commercial information if it is of a "confidential" nature and/or if the release of the information will harm the competitive position of the company or discourage commercial contracting with the government. But, freedom of information laws do not contain definitions of what information falls within these parameters.

The difference between the national policies rests on how this undefined exception is interpreted. In some nations the mere claim or belief that information is of a confidential commercial character is sufficient to provide a basis for denying access to contracts for public services. In other nations only a very limited amount of commercial information is considered to be of a confidential nature, denials of access must be justified on very specific grounds, and public service contracts are public record.

Where a broad cloak of secrecy is still in effect, it is a vestige of a long historical concept that places government in the role of master rather than servant of the public. Significant reforms have taken place within the past few decades and the EU has started to adopt standards which apply to EU government and proceedings. However, it has not adopted freedom of information rules that are applicable to member states, with the exception of rules applicable to access to environmental information.

Most Central and Eastern European nations have adopted constitutional provisions which provide for a right to information and access to public records. Commonly these provisions contain exceptions or qualifications that may be used to severely limit their scope. Examples include exceptions for "the rights of others" or "economic interests of the state". Others require that the party interested in obtaining the information must have a particular interest, such as a "sufficient legal interest" or the information must "concern" them. Some of the constitutions require implementing legislation defining the scope of exemptions or setting forth the procedures for availability of information. Typically, such legislation has not been adopted. (Appendix A contains the freedom of information sections in the constitutions of CEE nations.

Under the Czech Constitution (Article 17), the following is stated:

(1)   {...} the right to information is guaranteed;

(4)   {...} and the right to seek and disseminate information may be limited by law in the case of measures essential in a democratic society for protecting the rights and freedoms of others, the security of the State, public security, public health, and morality;

(5)   Organs of the State and of local self-government shall provide in an appropriate manner information on their activity. The conditions and the form of implementation of this duty shall be set by law.

A 1998 commentary on the Czech law noted that statutory limits to access to information included state secrecy, economic or professional secrets and that the rules for "secret information" and "commercial secrecy" were vague.[22] In 1999, the Czech Republic passed a new freedom of information law. During the debates over the new law, opponents argued that city officials would be flooded with requests for copies of the contracts; but since its passage the flood has not emerged. The public officials interviewed indicated that contracts executed after the adoption of this law are made accessible to the public, but that earlier contracts are not covered. 'Trade secrets' are an exception to the right to freedom of information. In order for information to qualify as a trade secret all of the following conditions must be met: it has to deal with:

a)   facts of trade, industrial or technical nature related to the company;

b)   it must have potential value;

c)   it cannot be commonly available in business circles;

d)   the entrepreneur desires that it be kept confidential.

Information submitted in price setting proceedings is not considered to be public record. For example, in accordance with national law, an office of energy regulation has to review the power over district heat prices set by local companies. In cases where prices exceed specified levels, rate increases must be justified under a cost and asset value formula. The proceedings for making these determinations are not public and the cost information submitted is not public record.

Under the Hungarian Constitution (Article 61) "... everyone has the right to ... information of public interest..." Furthermore, under the Hungarian Law "On the Protection of Personal Data and Accessibility of Data of Public Interest",[23] the authorities are required to grant access for anyone to the data of "public interest", unless the data is specifically restricted by law.[24] There is no specific exemption in that law for commercial information. Furthermore, "data of public interest" is broadly defined to include: "any information under processing by an authority performing state or local self-government functions or other public duties, except for personal data."[25] Another section of the law states that: "Access to data of public interest may not be restricted to protect those data of a person acting on behalf of the authority which are conjunctive to his or her duty."[26]

Hungary also has a separate business secrets law, which protects "any fact, information, solution or data, connected to economic activities, the secrecy of which is in the reasonable interest of the entitled party."[27] Its laws do not set forth the relation between the Accessibility of Data and the Business Secret laws. In the course of interviews in the spring of 1998 in over ten cities, in the majority of the cases, subject to the exception of a substantial minority, local officials took the position that contracts by public entities with private companies were not public records and therefore, citizens do not have the right to obtain such documents. In some cases, inquiries as to whether such records were public made local officials rather uncomfortable. In some cases, mixed responses were given; the local official responded that in principle the contracts were public, but that in practice nobody had requested copies of contracts and they were not given out. In other cases, such requests were viewed as unreasonable. As in the case of public contracts, submissions used for public price settings are not treated as public records. The most significant example of this practice is that submissions to the Ministry of Transport, Communication, and Water Management, are used for setting the water price for the five regional companies, which set rates for 45% of the country, are not accessible under current practice. Furthermore, the submissions that are used to justify local tariff subsidies for hundreds of water districts are not accessible.

In opinions regarding the relationship between public funds and private business, the national ombudsman has stated that "The transparency and controllability of the privatization processes, as public interest, takes precedence over the private interest of protection of business secrets."[28] In November 1998, in a case involving a challenge to the Transport Ministry's decision to keep a highway concession agreement secret, the ombudsman commented that:

> Citizens and their organizations can only keep a check on the activity of the state if they have sufficient information on their operation. {...} State or municipal organs learn business secrets very often when they deal with asset management and when they manage public funds. In these cases the principle of publicity has priority, since the utilization of public finances should be transparent. Since free access to information is a constitutional right, the right to have business secrets can not come before that. Private companies that apply for state or municipal subsidies or enter for a competition for subsidies or companies that have business relations with the state and municipality where public finances are involved, or if they manage public assets, often are exposed to the restriction of the right to have business secrets.[29]

Subsequent to the ombudsman's decision, the Ministry of Transportation has still refused to release the contract. (Appendix B contains the complete text of the Ombudsman's decision.)

The Romanian Constitution sets forth the right to public information in broad terms. It states that: *(Article 31)*

(1) A person's right of access to any information of public interest cannot be restricted.

(2) The public authorities, according to their competence, shall be bound to provide forcorrect information for citizens in public affairs and matters of personal interest.

Under the national law governing local authorities which has expired, one of the duties of local secretaries was to make sure that "decisions and orders of general interest are made public," including "abstracts or duplicates of any act in the council's archives".[30] But these provisions contained an exception for documents with "a secret character under the law". Up to this time, "secret character under the law" has not been defined by any law. According to author-investigated information, as a matter of practice, public contracts and related information are kept secret. In the draft of the new law on local public services every person has the right to "access to information about the local public services" and the "right to be consulted, directly or by means of non-governmental organizations of the users, while the decisions, strategies, and the regulations on the activities related to local public services are drawn and adopted." In 1996, freedom of information legislation was introduced in the parliament, but was not adopted.[31] Since then, access to information in public contracts has become a major public issue in reaction to the execution of a secret contract between the national telephone provider (RomTelecom) and a Greek firm. As of August 2001 a new freedom of information law had been passed by the parliament but had not been signed into law.

In March 2001, a shadow was cast over freedom of information in Romania by the introduction of a broad law for the protection of "classified information". Classified information includes:

> economic information which {...} affects national economic interests. Public officials and citizens who fail to turn over or fail to report their knowledge of such information to the national authorities.

The government indicated that the passage of such a law was necessary in order to join NATO. Subsequently, the Romanian Supreme Court struck down the law on the basis of procedural defects in adoption. The draft freedom of information law sets forth a basic right to access to information which contains the typical exemptions from public access. In addition to these laws, the procurement law contains specific provisions regarding public access which requires that the authorities maintain the confidentiality of commercial secrets.[32] More importantly, all access to the information in contracts is effectively cut off by a provision in the implementing regulations which contains a model contract which states that a contract may not be released to the public without the consent of both contracting parties.

Under the Slovakian constitution:

> State bodies and their territorial self-administration bodies are under an obligation to provide information on their activities in an appropriate manner The conditions and manner of execution will be specified by law.[33]

In 1998, the secrecy of a Bratislava contract with a foreign company (Siemans) for the provision of street lighting became a major public issue. Also, in recent years, public reactions to the policies of the Meclar regime led to strong pressures for more open government after its fall from power. On 1 January 2001, a new free access to information act become effective. That act covers:

c)   information obtained through public funds or relating to the use of public funds or state or municipal property,

d)   {...}information under Sec. 3, Sec. 2. [... information pertaining to the management of public funds and utilization of state property or the property of municipalities;

and [information] on the content, performance [of any concluded agreements] and activities carried out on the basis of any concluded agreement.]

The Act contains the standard exemption for any information "classified as a trade secret".[34] (Commercial Code Sections 17–20). However, "Disclosure of the following information shall not be deemed as a violation or jeopardizing a trade secret: ... information obtained through public funds or relating to the use of public funds or state or municipal property."[35] In the course of interviews, some public officials took the position that contracts for public services are available to the public as a result of the new freedom of information law and provided copies of the contracts, while others maintained that they were confidential. One city official took the position that contracts between the city and private companies were public record but that a contract governing the relationship between a municipal partner and a private partner in a joint venture was a commercial secret.

The Romanian Concession law,[36] which is modeled after the French concession act, contains extensive requirements on the terms and conditions of a concession contract. In addition, the law requires that the initiation of a concession has to be accompanied by an opportunity study which contains a statement of:

1)   the reasons of an economic, financial, social, and environmental nature which justify the concession,

2)   the necessary investments for modernization and extension,

3)   the estimated period of the concession,

4)   the minimum rent.[37]

The contract is subject to the norms set up in a frame document to be approved by the government.

3.1 Transparency in Western Countries

Some nations, including Canada, Australia, Sweden, and the U.S. have developed strong transparency requirements, which include public access to public contracts. In these nations transparency is a fundamental right in the law and in practice. Exemptions are narrowly interpreted and some of the access laws provide that public interest in access may override the commercial exemption. Public contracts and information submitted to price setting agencies are both readily and easily available to the public.

Western European Declarations and Legislation on access to public documents contain broad statements of a principle of public access, which are subject to broad exceptions. In the past decade, EU nations have been moving towards stronger freedom of infomation requirements. Access to public documents has been an area of increasing concern in recent decades.[38] In 1982, the Council of Europe Committee of Ministers adopted a "Declaration on the Freedom of Expression and Information".[39] It states that they "...seek to achieve the ... following objectives: ... the pursuit of an open information policy in the public sector, including access to information, in order to enhance the individual's understanding of, and his ability to discuss freely political, social, economic and cultural matters; ..."[40]

The EC Code of Conduct Concerning Public Access to Council and Commission Documents, which was adopted in 1993, sets forth the General Principle that "The public will have the widest possible access to documents held by the Commission and the Council".[41] The Code requires that decisions of its institutions on requests for documents must be made within 30 days, that the grounds for a refusal must be set forth in writing, and that means of redress are available through judicial proceedings and complaints to the ombudsman.

Exceptions to Access under EC Code of Conduct

The institutions will refuse access to any document whose disclosure could undermine {...}

– the protection of the public interest (public security, ... monetary stability), ...

– the protection of commercial and industrial secrecy,

– the protection of the Community's financial interests,

– the protection of confidentiality as requested by the natural or legal persons that supplied the information or as required by the legislation of the Member State that supplied the information. {...}"

However, EU standards for freedom of information of member states are limited to environmental information.[42] The applicable directive contains the standard exemption for "commercial and industrial confidentiality." Pursuant to this directive, the member nations have adopted legislation specifically for access to environmental information.

Under Austrian law, public agency contracts are not public record. However, a losing bidder in a tender has the right to see the contract that is made with the winner of the tender.[43]

Under French law governing access to administrative documents,[44] there is an exception for commercial and industrial secrets.[45]A 'Commission d'Acces aux Documents Administratifs' (the Commission for Access of Administrative Documents) (CADA) is responsible for administering the law and making administrative determinations about access to particular documents. Its commentary on the French act notes the scope of the exception is not precise and that it has not been defined by the courts.[46] However, the 1999 annual report of the Commission states that all the financial elements, including the detailed prices, contained in a contract with a public agency, are public record because they reflect elements of the cost of the service to the public.[47] (In contrast, in the case of offers that are not accepted, only the global price offered is public record.) The report lists cases in which it has ruled that concession contracts are public record.[48]

115

Germany has not adopted freedom of information legislation, except within its environmental legislation.[49]

In Great Britain, the public access issue has been the subject of wide discussion and pressures for reform. In 2000, Great Britain passed a new freedom of information act.[50] The act contains an exemption for "trade secrets" and for cases in which disclosure would "prejudice the commercial interests of any person (including the public authority holding it.)".[51]

Pursuant to the new act, the government is drafting a "Code of Practice on the Discharge of the Functions of Public Authorities…" In the draft version, public authorities are directed to severely limit the use of confidentiality clauses and only accept such provisions when their use is for "good reasons and can be justified by the Commissioner".

Code of Practice on the Discharge of the Functions of Public Authorities
under Part I of the Freedom of Information Act of 2000

24.   When entering into contracts public authorities should refuse to include contractual terms which purport to restrict the disclosure of information held by the authority and relating to the contract beyond the restrictions permitted in the Act. In particular, when entering into contracts, as when receiving information from third parties more generally, public authorities should not agree to hold information 'in confidence' which is not in fact confidential in nature.

25.   Public authorities when entering into contracts with non-public authority contractors may be under pressure to accept confidentiality clauses so that information relating to the terms of the contract, its value and performance will be exempt from disclosure. Public authorities should, whenever commercially viable, endeavor to obtain the agreement of the non-public authority contractor that no such confidentiality can be set up against a request for the disclosure of such information.

26.   Any acceptance of such confidentiality provisions must be for good reasons and capable of being justified by the Commissioner.

27.   Public authorities should not impose terms of secrecy on contractors unless the information concerned would be exempt within the terms of the Act. However, except where paragraph 28 below applies, it is for the public authority to disclose information pursuant to the Act, and not the contractor. The public authority may need to protect from disclosure by the contractor information which would be exempt from disclosure under the Act, by appropriate contractual terms.

Under the former British Freedom of Information law, there was a non-statutory *Code of Practice on Access to Government Information*, which included an exemption for "commercial confidences, trade secrets or intellectual property whose unwarranted disclosure would harm the competitive position of a third party". The "Guidance on Interpretation" issued by the Cabinet Office advised decision makers to ask three questions when deciding whether to withhold commercial information:

(i) is the information {...} a trade secret, a commercial confidence, or intellectual property? The Code suggests adopting the Alberta *Trade Secret Act 1986* definition of a trade secret. If the answer is "no" then the exemption does not apply. If the answer is "yes" {...}

(ii) would its disclosure be likely to harm the competitive position of the subject or source of the information? If the answer is "yes", disclosure is unwarranted unless there is an overriding public interest in disclosure. If the answer is "no" {...}

(iii) would its disclosure be likely to prejudice the future supply of information to the government? If the answer is "yes" then disclosure is unwarranted.[52]

Some agencies, including the national agency which regulates water prices (OFWAT), provides public access to cost submissions which are used to justify price increases.

Under Swedish law, "access to official documents may be restricted only if the restriction is necessary having regard to ... 5. the public economic interest; 6. the protection of {...} economic conditions of private subjects."[53] The term 'document' is broadly defined to include any document in the possession of a public authority.[54] All documents are public unless exempted by the Secrecy Act. In regards to commercial information that act exempts: A person's business or management conditions, inventions or research results, if it can be assumed that the person concerned would suffer loss should the information be disclosed. However, the act also permits the government to override the secrecy provision "if the government deems it important that the information is provided." As a matter of practice, contracts for services are made public.

Under the Canadian freedom of information act, public contracts are treated as public records The exemption section of its legislation states that:

> Subject to this section, the head of a government institution shall refuse to disclose any record requested under this Act that contains trade secrets of a third party; financial, commercial, scientific or technical information that is confidential information supplied to a government institution by a third party and is treated consistently in a confidential manner by the third party; information the disclosure of which could reasonably be expected to result in material financial loss or gain to, or could reasonably be expected to prejudice the competitive position of, a third party; information the disclosure of which could reasonably be expected to interfere with contractual or other negotiations of a third party.[55]

As in Sweden, there is a provision which allows the public interest to override a commercial exemption. Judicial analysis of the exemption section illustrates the narrow interpretation of the scope of the exemption. One decision notes application of the financial information exemption "require[s] a reasonable expectation of probable harm {...} speculation of mere possibility or harm does not meet that standard".[56]

Under U.S. laws, contracts by public entities are public record. The federal Freedom of Information Act contains an exemption for "trade secrets and commercial or financial information obtained from a person and privileged or confidential..."[57] State laws, which govern contracts by state and local governments, contain similar provisions. Typically the commercial exemptions are interpreted narrowly.

In a leading decision "trade secret" was defined as:

> a secret, commercially valuable plan, formula, process or device that is used for making, preparing, compounding, or processing of trade commodities and that can be said to be the end product of either innovation or substantial effort.[58]

Generally, commercial information that is used to demonstrate that a company has the financial resources to undertake a project or to protect trade secrets is exempted from public access. The common judicial test of whether a government agency can refuse to disclose business information is whether the release of the information would be damaging to the business or would discourage future competition for public contracts. For discussion of the commercial exemptions under the laws of Australia, Canada, France, Great Britain, Ireland, New Zealand, Sweden, and the United States see Baxter, Richard, "Commercial Confidentiality", *Freedom of Information—Resolving Disputes* (1995)[59]

3.2 Transparency and Public Participation in the Drafting of Contracts

Research in Hungary revealed that contracts with local governments are commonly drafted by companies that win a tender without serious review by the local government and without the assistance of an attorney reviewing the contract and negotiating on behalf of the local government.

Possible measures to improve the quality of contracts include:

1. Creation of local government subcommittees with responsibility for drafting contracts,
2. Public hearings on the content of proposed contracts,
3. Inclusion of experts in the contract drafting process,
4. Requirements that the contract be developed before the tendering process.

A Romanian lawyer who specializes in municipal contracts stated that contracting out was typically characterized by a lack of performance standards and monitoring. A proposal for the creation of water board modeled after the British Water Board (OFWAT) includes the provision of free technical assistance to cities in the preparation of concession contracts.

Opponents of public access to contracts and price setting information claim that public access discourages firms from entering into contracts with public agencies. Among their concerns is that business will be afraid to submit business information because it will be used municipal councilors who are competitors or who are likely to share information with competitors. However, there does not seem any evidence to support this conclusion and the experiences of nations with public access to public contracts have not been marked by any lack of commercial interest in obtaining public contracts due to such rules.

On the other hand, there is no question that maintaining the secrecy of public contracts contributes to corruption, lowers performance requirements for drafting such contracts by shielding them from public view, and undercuts the credibility of the contracting out process.

4. CONFLICT OF INTEREST LAWS

> *Just as it is impossible not to taste honey or poison that one may find at the tip of one's tongue, so it is impossible for one dealing with government funds not to taste, at least a little bit, of the King's wealth.*

> Kautilya, Prime Minister
> of a state in Northern India

4.1 Conflicts of Interest and the Law in CEE Nations

Throughout the CEE, interviewees stated that conflicts of interest are standard in the public contracting process. Typically, members of City Assemblies vote on contracts in cases when they also have an interest in the enterprises that are awarded the contracts. Conversely, interviewees recounted instances in which city assembly members opposed contracting out because they were on the board of the publicly controlled company which currently provided the service.

Conflict of interest laws are spread among laws governing national and local governments and commercial companies. In addition, national procurement laws prevent the participation of persons in the selection process of the procurement procedure with an interest in the outcome of the procedure. Sometimes the scope of the national laws is limited to a few specifically mentioned types of conflicts.

While broad principles about the impropriety of conflict of interests are present in national laws, conflict of interest legislation is characterized by a lack of any penalties and/or enforcement mechanisms for violations. None of the interviewees mentioned any instances in which public officials of any type had been penalized for conflict of interest violations or of cases in which contracts had been annulled due to such conflicts of interest. At the same time, there is general public disgust with such conflicts of interest.

The ineffectiveness of the national laws may be evidenced by the fact within each country widely differing answers were given about whether there even were conflict of interest laws and/or their scope. Commonly, interviewees who were knowledgeable about public law and policy stated that there were no conflict of interest laws. It seems that the laws which do exist act as theoretical statements of public objectives without much real significance.

Furthermore, some interviewees stated that persons who claimed that particular public officials had conflicts of interests faced the threat of lawsuits for defamation. After making such a claim, a deputy mayor of a major Polish City was subject to a defamation claim, which took five years to resolve. In the end, the former deputy mayor prevailed in national supreme court. at a cost that most people could not bear.

Conflict of interest laws can provide some relief by prohibiting direct and open ties between the decision making authorities and parties that are awarded contracts. Obviously, they cannot prevent secret ties. However, interviewees repeatedly indicated that such legislation would be very useful, even though it may be circumvented.

While this section provides describes the conflict of interest laws in the CEE, the EU, and the US, the real differences are in the political climate which determines whether or not the laws are enforced.

The Romanian procurement law addresses conflicts of interest in the procurement process by prohibiting the following interested parties from participating in a Procurement Evaluation Commission decision[60]:

a)   a spouse or relative to the third degree of one of the tenderers,

b)   persons who in the last three years have worked for or signed a contract with one of the tendering parties or what have participated in its Council of Administration or a leading administration body.

c)   persons who hold shares in a significant percentage of the capital of one of the tenderers.

Furthermore, parties that participated in the draft of the tender announcement and/or selection of tender criteria may not participate in the tender procedure and the party that is awarded the contract may not employ anyone who has served on the Evaluation Commission. Similar provisions are contained in Hungary's procurement law.[61] One district of Bratislava indicated that it requires that members of procurement selection committees must sign statements indicating that they do not have any conflict of interest.

Interviewees in Romania indicated that there were no conflict of interest laws other than the provisions in the procurement law. In addition, persons who claim that a public official has a conflict of interest but fail to prove that claim may be subject to significant sanctions.

Czech interviewees stated that there were no real conflict of interest laws. However, the Czech administrative procedure law contains general and broad conflict of interest exclusions, which provide for the disqualification of an administrative authority's employees or members. It applies to situations in which "unprejudiced" consideration may be "doubted owing to his relationship to the matter, parties to the proceedings or their representatives".[62] Furthermore, any party to the proceedings is required to report any basis for disqualifying themselves or other employees which they are aware of.

The Public Service Law describes conflict of interest in very broad terms. It states that:

> in the performance of his or her office, a public servant must proceed in a responsible manner, must respect and protect human dignity and human rights and freedoms: must avoid anything which would generate doubts regarding his or her objectivity in protecting the public interest.[63]

The views of knowledgeable persons that there are no conflict of interest laws in the Czech Republic, notwithstanding the above quoted sections, demonstrates the dormant state of the laws in this area.

Various Hungarian laws include provisions against conflicts of interest. For example, the Local Government Act excludes participation in decision making in a case where a person (or their relative) is personally affected by a matter.[64] A Civil Service law prohibits civil servants from pursuing activities which would endanger objectivity and impartiality in public service.[65]

Interviewees in Slovakia had different views about the state of the law, ranging from views that there was no conflict of interest law, that the law only applied to state employees, to the view that the law applied to municipal employees.

4.2 Conflict of Interest Laws in the EU and the US

In recent years in the EU, conflict of interest laws have been the subject of widespread national legislative activity and EC discussions as a part of the anti-corruption campaigns of the region.[66] In France and Great Britain, national agencies have been created for the purpose of enforcing compliance by local government officials with conflict of interest laws. Also, the laws commonly require local officials to disclose their assets.

The EC "Model code of conduct for public officials", promulgated by the Committee of Ministers to Member States on Codes of Conduct for Public Officials, , includes the following conflict of interest standards:[67]

Article 13—Conflict of Interest

1. Conflict of interest arises from a situation in which the public official has a private interest which is such as to influence, the impartial and objective performance of his or her official duties.

2. The public official's private interest includes any advantage to himself or herself, to his or her family, close relatives, friends and persons or organizations with whom he or she has or has had business or political relations. It includes also any liability, whether financial or civil, relating thereto.

3. Since the public official is usually the only person who knows whether he or she is in that situation, the public official has a personal responsibility to:

    1. To be alert to any actual or potential conflict of interest; take steps to avoid such conflict;

    2. To disclose to his or her supervisor any such conflict as soon as he or she becomes aware of it;

    3. To comply with any final decision to withdraw from the situation or to divest himself or herself of the advantage causing the conflict.

4. Whenever required to do so, the public official should declare whether or not he or she has a conflict of interest.

5. Any conflict of interest declared by a candidate to the public service or to a new post in the public service should be resolved before appointment.

The public official who occupies a position in which his or her personal or private interests are likely to be affected by his or her official duties should, as lawfully required, declare upon appointment, at regular intervals thereafter and whenever any changes occur in the nature of those interests.

Article 15—Incompatible outside interests

1. The public official should not engage in any activity or transaction or acquire any position or function, whether paid or unpaid, that is incompatible with or detracts from the proper performance of his or her duties as a public official. Where it is not clear whether any activity is compatible, he or she should seek advice from his or her superior.

2. Subject to the provisions of the law, the public official should be required to notify and seek the approval of his or her public service employer to carry out certain

activities, whether paid or unpaid, or to accept certain positions or functions outside his or her public service employment.

Great Britain adopted extensive conflict of interest legislation in 2000.[68] The Act provides for a national standards of conduct board, with investigative powers and adjudicatory powers, including the power to suspend officials from their public positions. In addition, the law and requires that each locality adopt a code of conduct and a local standards committee.

French law provides for an inter-ministerial inquiry committee which is charged with assuring the regularity and impartiality of public contracting procedures[69] and contains strong sanctions against violations of conflict of interest standards. Penalties of up to $100,000 and $200,000 are included.

The Danish conflict of interest law is very broad. It requires exclusion from participation in all public matters where there is a potential financial or personal interest. Furthermore, it requires exclusion in the event of "circumstances {...} are likely to lead to any doubt about such persons impartiality."[70] Any person who has notice of the types of circumstances covered by the conflict of interest provisions is required to notify a superior as soon as possible. The Act does contain exceptions in the case that "no risk may be assumed to exist that the decision to be made may be affected by extraneous considerations." or "it would be impossible or attended with substantial difficulties or misgivings to arrange for another person to act in his stead in considering the matter."

In the US, conflicts of interest in local governments are covered by state laws.[71] Typically, these laws contain broad definitions of conflict of interest; they require public office holders to submit disclosures of their assets; specify a time period during which former public employees cannot represent private companies before the former employing agency; provide for substantial penalties; and establish independent commissions which are responsible for the enforcement of the laws. In the US, unlike Europe, financial disclosures which public officials are required to submit are accessible to the general public. U.S. law review articles contain detailed discussions of the practical strengths and weakness of the laws and their specific provisions.[72]

The US, laws expressly prohibit public officials from using their office or employment to obtain any financial gain for themselves, members of their family, or businesses with which their associated. Public officials are prohibited from accepting or soliciting anything of value if their vote would be influenced.

Other types of provisions include:

- prohibitions of substantial severance payments by private companies to employees prior to their assuming public positions;

- provisions which enable private parties, as well as the enforcement agency, to bring civil court actions;

- protections of 'whistleblowers' (public employees who report violations of the laws by their superiors).

The State Ethics Commissions typically have responsibility for:

1) conducting investigations and making determinations of these investigations;

2) insuring the filing and public availability of statements of financial interest;

3) issuing advise and opinions to persons about their obligations under the law.

5. CONCLUSION

In the CEE nations which were surveyed in this study, public policy and regulation in regards to contracting out public services is marked by severe shortcomings. A substantial portion of contracting out is exempt from competitive procurement requirements, contracts are widely treated as secret, and conflicts of interest are largely unregulated. Under these circumstances, the public has little reason to have faith or respect for the contracting out process and the essential elements of public participation and scrutiny are lost.

Reform in this area should include the following:

1. All contracts for public services (except for very small contracts) should be subject to a competitive bidding process.

2. Sales and leases of public facilities and sales of ownership shares in public facilities should be subject to the same competitive requirements as contracting out of public services.

3. All public contracts with private companies for the provision of public services should be accessible to the public (with very narrow exceptions for specified portions of contracts based on exceptional circumstances).

4. The drafting of public contracts should be an open process subject to public input and review.

5. Information submitted in price setting procedures should be public record.

6. Conflict of Interest Laws should include:

    a. Broad definitions of conflicts of interest;

    b. Requirements for disclosure of assets by public officials that are open to the public;

    c. Prohibitions against representation of private companies by former public officials for specified time periods;

    d. Protections of 'whistleblowers';

e.   Penalties for violations of the law;

f.   Independent national commissions responsible for enforcing conflict of interest laws.

Badly needed public investments in public service provision may not be undertaken or may be contracted out because otherwise they would be unaffordable. However, the types of reforms proposed here do not require public expenditures, and they provide possibilities for greatly improving the investments in public services which are undertaken.

APPENDIX A

Text of Constitutional Provisions and Legislation Covering Freedom of Information, and Exceptions to Freedom of Information Requirements (Including Commercial Secrets Legislation) in Central and East European Nations

Albania

Albanian Constitution, Article 23

1.   The right to information is guaranteed.

2.   Everyone has the right, in compliance with the law, to get information about the activity of state organs, as well as of persons who exercise state functions.

Bulgaria

Bulgarian Constitution, Article 41 (Sec. 2)

Citizens shall be entitled to obtain information from state bodies and agencies on any matter of legitimate interest to them which is not a state or official secret and does not affect the rights of others.

Czech Republic

Czech Constitution, Article 17

(1)   ... and the right to information are guaranteed, ...

(4)   ... and the right to seek and disseminate information may be limited by law in the case of measures essential in a democratic society for protecting the rights and freedoms of others, the security of the State, public security, public health, and morality,

(5)   Organs of the State and of local self-government shall provide in an appropriate manner information on their activity. The conditions and the form of implementation of this duty shall be set by law.

Estonia

Estonian Constitution, Article 44 (Sec.2)

At the request of Estonian citizens, and to the extent and in accordance with procedures determined by law, all state and local government authorities and their officials shall be obligated to provide information on their work, with the exception of information which is forbidden by law to be divulged, and information which is intended for internal use only.

Latvia

Latvian Constitution, Article 100

Everyone has the right to freedom of expression which includes the right to freely receive, keep and distribute information ....

Lithuania

Lithuanian Constitution Article 25 (Sec.5)

Citizens shall have the right to obtain any available information which concerns them from State agencies in the manner established by law.

Macedonia (FYRM)

Macedonian Constitution, Article 16 (Sec.3)

Free access to information and the freedom of reception and transmission of information are guaranteed

Poland

Under the Polish Constitution the right to obtain access to public documents is subject to the "Limitations ... *imposed by statute* .... to protect freedoms and rights of other persons and economic subjects, public order, security or important economic interests of the State." However, efforts to include a right for business secrets in the Constitution were rejected.

The Constitution states:

Polish Constitution (Article 61)

(1) A citizen shall have the right to obtain information on the activities of organs of public authority as well as persons discharging public functions. Such right shall also include receipt of information on the activities of self-governing economic or professional organs and other persons or organizational units relating to the field in which they perform the duties of public authorities and manage communal assets or property of the State Treasury.

(2) The right to obtain information shall ensure access to documents and entry to sittings of collective organs of public authority formed by universal elections, with the opportunity to make sound and visual recordings.

(3) Limitations upon the rights referred to in Paragraphs (1) and (2), may be imposed by statute solely to protect freedoms and rights of other persons and economic subjects, public order, security or important economic interests of the State.

(4) The procedure for the provision of information, referred to in Paragraphs (1) and (2) above shall be specified by statute, and regarding the House of Representatives (Sejm) and the Senate by their rules of procedure.

Although this article directs the legislature to adopt a statute governing procedures for access to information, no statute has been adopted up to this time. Also, no limitations in access have been adopted by statute. Nevertheless, according to the various sources contacted, contracts are regarded as secret.

Romania[73]

Romanian Constitution (Article 31)

(1) A person's right of access to any information of public interest cannot be restricted.

(2) The public authorities, according to their competence, shall be bound to provide for correct information for citizens in public affairs and matters of personal interest.

Russia

Russian Constitution, Article 29 (Sec.4)

Everyone shall have the right to seek, get, transfer, produce and disseminate information by any lawful means. The list of information constituting the state secret shall be established by the federal law.

Slovakia

Slovakian Constitution Article 26 (Sec. 5)

State bodies and their territorial self-administration bodies are under an obligation to provide information on their activities in an appropriate manner .... The conditions and manner of execution will be specified by law.

Slovenia

Slovenian Constitution (Article 39, Sec.2)

Except in such circumstances as are laid down by statute, each person shall have the right to obtain information of a public nature, provided he can show sufficient legal interest as determined by statute.

Ukraine

Ukrainian Constitution (Article 34)

... Every person has the right to collect, keep, use and disseminate information ...
The execution of these rights may be limited by law in the interests of national security, territorial integrity or the public order for the purposes of preventing disturbances or crimes, to protect the health of the population, to protect the reputations or rights of other people, to prevent the announcement of information received confidentially, or to support the authority and impartiality of justice.

APPENDIX B

Decision by Hungarian Ombudsman
—Public Access to Highway Concession Contract (1998)

Data Protection Commissioner

recommendation

relating the publicity of concession contracts

I.   Launching an Inquiry

The president of the Legal and Advocacy Protection Committee of the Hungarian Automobile Club presented a petition to the Data Protection Commissioner asking for a position to be taken in connection with the content of the concession contract concluded between the Ministry of Transportation, Telecommunications and Water Management and the First Hungarian Concession Motorway Rt. (ELMKA) for the construction and operation of M1/M5 motorways. The petitioner holds the opinion that the business interest of the economic company and that of the Ministry concluding the contract can not be more important than the principle of having access to data of public interest. A similar opinion is aired by the president of ELMKA published in an article published in the monthly 'Autósélet' and attached by the petitioner. In this article, the president says: Issues in connection with the public service should be transparent, so the contract is practically open to everyone.

In connection with this issue I asked the Minister of Transportation, Telecommunications and Water Management to take position. The public administration State Secretary trusted by the Minister declared that the concession contract is a legal entity, not a fact, therefore it can not be considered as data, so the 1992. LXIII. act on the protection of personal data and publicity of public data is not applicable. According to his view, the concession contracts should be handled as any other contracts: the content of any contract can be known to a third party only if this is not excluded in the contract for business reasons.

Since the winners and creditors of the concession tender for motorways M1/M5 insist that the content of the contract should be handled as a business secret, the State Secretary is of the opinion that the Ministry applied the right step when denied publicity.

II.   The Legal Background of the Case

1.   Section 10, paragraph (2) of the Constitution states that the exclusive property of the state and the circle of exclusive economic activities of the state is defined by law.

2.   The preamble of Act XVI of 1991 on Concessions (hereinafter: ConAct) sets forth the following: 'one possible way of way of efficiently operating the property exclusively owned by the state, or the local government or the associations of local governments, and of the exercise of the activities referred to the exclusive competence of the state or the local government is the assignment of all these by way of a contract of concession'.

The aim of contracts of concession is to assure the right to pursue activities. In the Act, there is a list of activities that the state is obliged to announce and then operate through concession. The concession contract can apply not only to the managing of already existing assets, but also for assets that will be the result of a future investment. One way of renouncing the right to operate is that the contracting party partially or solely undertakes the financing of big value investments where the capital requirement is very big.

The ConAct contains the following about the publicity of the concession procedure:

" Section 4, subsection (1) The state or the local government shall invite tenders, with the exception of the aforesaid under Section 12, subsection (2), for the conclusion of a *contract of concession. Tenders - except when national defense or security reasons necessitate a closed tender, are open to the public. In this case Law-Decree No. 19 of 1987 on Tenders need not be applied.*

Section 8, subsection (1) Invitation for open tenders shall be published in at least two dailies of nation-wide circulation, and, in the case of local government, in the local daily paper at least 30 days prior to the first day of the period of submitting applications. In the case of a closed tender, the invitees shall be invited to tender concurrently and directly.

(2)   The invitation for tenders shall contain the aspects of evaluation and as to the activity subject to concession, it shall

a)   list any other related activities

b)   define the period of concession to be granted

c)   define the geographical-administrative unit in which the activity is to be pursued

d)   define the legal and financial conditions upon which the activity is to be pursued

e)   define the conditions upon premature termination of the contract of concession,

f)   contain information as to the rights of the state (local government) concerning the supervising of the terms of concession,

g) contain information as to who has the right to pursue activity subject to concession in the area affected by tender, at the time of inviting for tenders, and whether the invitor tends to grant the right of pursuing the activity subject to concession to other economic organisations during the term of concession.

3) If necessary, the tender shall also contain:

a) professional conditions pertaining to the pursuit of the activity, which exceed or depart from, those described by legal rules or standards (e.g., environmental protection, health protection),

b) conditions relating to the employment of domestic labour force and domestic entrepreneurs and suppliers, in the course of the exercise of the activity,

c) the minimum amount of the concession fee,

d) rules and collaterals with regard to the delivery and return of the property owned exclusively by the government (primary assets of the local government) provided the pursuit of the activity subject to concession requires the assignment of the possession of this property

e) information as to whether the sectoral Act prescribes parliamentary approval for the conclusion of a contract of concession,

f) the rules of price calculation of the licensed activity, including the methods and principles of defining and changing the price and charge,

g) any other information that the invitor deems necessary."

As to the evaluation of the tenders and the publicity of the concluded contracts of concession, no rules are mentioned in the ConAct or the Act I of 1988.

Section 19 sets forth that *"Unless this act provides otherwise, the provisions of the Civil Code shall apply to a contract of concession"*.

3. Act LVII of 1996, subsection (4) on unfair market behaviour and the prohibition on the restriction of competition states that " it is forbidden to acquire and utilise business secrets in an unfair way, or to inform non- competent persons about business secrets or to publicise business secrets.

4. Act IV of 1959, subsection 81 on Civil Code sets forth:*" Persons who violate mail secret, who—in an unauthorised way—get hold of private, company or business secret and reveal it or abuse in any way, violate rights related to persons.*

5. Section 300, subsection (1) of Act IV of 1978 on Penal Code sets forth that "a person who in an unauthorised way abuses, publicises business secrets to benefit by it, thus causing material damage, is committing felony and is subject to imprisonment up to 3 years.

6. Section 61, subsection (1) sets forth *" in the Hungarian Republic everyone has the right to express an open opinion, furthermore has the right to have and publicise public data."*

7.   Act LXIII of 1992 (hereinafter: Avtv.), Section 2, subsection (3) on the protection of personal data and the publicity of public data sets forth: *"data of public interest: data that do not constitute personal data and which are managed by persons or organisations providing state or local governmental services or any other services defined by law.*

Section 19 of Avtv sets forth the following: any organisation providing state or local governmental services or any other public services defined by law - including services in connection with its own management—, is obliged to provide precise and quick information to the public. It is the task of such organisations to assure that all public data managed by them are available to everyone except for cases when the data are declared by entitled entities to be state or service secrets, furthermore if the right to have access to a certain type of public data is restricted for reasons of national defence, national safety or for reasons of criminal prevention and prosecution, central financial or foreign exchange policy reasons or reasons related to foreign policy, relations with international organisations, court proceedings.

8.   Act IV of 1978, Section/A, subsection f) states that " *data managers who is secretive in connection with public data or falsifies public data, is committing felony that can lead to imprisonment up to 1 year, to public work or penalty. "*

III. Conclusions of the Inquiry

The right to have access to public data, the freedom of/for information is a basic constitutional right. Citizens and their organisations can only keep a check on the activity of the state or municipalities if they have sufficient information on their operation. In harmony with the data protection Act, the above mentioned organs are obliged to provide all possible information. As a general rule, they should assure the access to all data managed by them.

8/2 paragraph of the Constitution should be applied also for the freedom of information:

Examples for the legal restriction of information freedom is the Act on state secrets and service secrets, or the legal provisions concerning the protection of business secrets.

The right to have information on public data and the right to have business secret can contradict each other when organs with public activity have business relations with private companies, e.g. when they engage in a Public Procurement procedure, privatisation or concession or through the process of state and municipal property management or in cases when a state or municipal budgetary subsidy or favour is granted to a private company.

State or municipal organs learn business secrets very often when they deal with asset management and when they manage public funds. In these cases the principle of publicity has priority, since the utilisation of public finances and the state economy should be transparent. Since free access

133

to information is a constitutional right, the right to have business secrets can not come before that. Private companies that apply for state or municipal subsidies or enter for a competition for subsidies or companies that have business relations with the state and municipality where public finances are involved, or if they manage public assets, often are exposed to the restriction of the right to have business secrets.

Through concession the state, municipality renounces the right to carry out activities (there is an official, legal itemised list of these activities) temporarily. They conclude an onerous contract (consideration contract) which assures partial share of the market monopoly. The concession fee is usually transferred to the central budget. The ConAct declares:
When the state, municipality outsources the activity, the competition for the outsourcing activity is defined by law. Organisations or entrepreneurs should enter a competition that is defined by law and is public. The state, municipality can then select the best possible organisations or entrepreneurs that can serve the state, municipality and their community.

It is obvious from the data protection law and also from the above mentioned regulations of the concession law that when the state, municipality concludes a concession contract, it disposes over public funds. This explains why the content of this contract can not be considered as business secret, given the present system of information right.

In connection with the publicity of privatisation contracts and results of competitions for various budgetary subsidies and favours I have made some inquiries (528/A/1996., 503/K/1997., 227/K/1998. no. cases), and I still hold the opinion that based on the quoted laws, information found in a concession contract are public information and should be available to everyone.

Any agreement worded in the contract of concession concerning the obligation of the state, municipality to hold the content of the concession contract in secret contradicts Section 2, subsection(3) and section 19, of Avtv

Based on the quoted laws of Avtv. the obligation of publicity is binding not only for the content of the contract but also for the result of the competition. But at the same time, it is in the interest of those whose work did not win on the competition that their business data do not get publicised. The state, local government do not have the confidentiality obligation if the applicants reveal their business secrets when they appeal because they have complaints in connection with the results.

For legal safety it would be advisable to amend the ConAct so that all the participants: the state, municipality that announce the competition, the applicants that enter the competition would have clear knowledge as to what data can be public and what data should be public. (A good example for the clear, legal regulation is the 1996/I. Act on radio and television. The 96th paragraph (4th) section of this act defines one by one which data of a concession contract are subject to publicity after a concession contract was concluded for the provision of radio and television services).

IV.   Recommendation

Based on the above mentioned, I propose the following:

• I request the Minister of Transportation, Telecommunications and Water Management to assure that all data are public to the petitioners or any other parties that hold interest in connection with the content of the concession contract concluded between the Ministry of Transportation, Telecommunications and Water Management and the First Hungarian Concession Motorway Rt. (ELMKA) for the construction and operation of M1/M5 motorways.

• I request the Minister of Justice to initiate an amendment of act XVI of 1991 on concession so that interested participants could practice their constitutional right to have access to all public data.

Budapest, 1998. november

Dr. László Majtényi
Data Protection Commissioner

NOTES

1   Law on Concession, 1998, Law No. 219, Article 2.

2   Some interviewees noted that this approach for park maintenance improved performance by bringing about competition among the various park maintenance contractors to provide the best quality service. One district representative noted, with regret, that his district had significantly limited its future options in contracting street maintenance services, by virtue of its sale of its maintenance equipment to one company.

3   Interview with City Staff, February 2001.

4   Council Directive, 92/50/EEC, Article 1(a) (18 June 1992).

5   Arrowsmith, Sue, *Public Private Partnerships and the European Procurement Rules: EU Policies in Conflict?*, *Common Market Law Review* Vol. 37, 709, 713 (2000).

6   Council Directive, 92/50/EEC, Article 1(a)(iii) (18 June 1992).

7   Commission of the European Communities, *Commission Interpretative Communication on concessions under Community law*, Brussels, 12.4.2000, p. 15 (Official Journal of the European Communities, Vol. 43, 29 April 2000 (2000/C121/02), (http://europa.eu.int/comm./internal_market/en/publproc/general/conc2.htm).

8   Commission of the European Communities, *Commission Interpretative Communication on concessions under Community law*, Brussels, 12.4.2000, p. 16.

9   Hungary, Act XL of 1995, Introduction.

10   Ordinance No. 118. (1999).

11   Act 199 of 1994, published in English by Trade Links, , s.r.o., Prague (Miscellaneous Acts in 2000).

12   Act 199, Sec. 1 (r) and (s).

13   Section 37.

14   Section 37(2).

15   Act XII of 1995.

16   Act XL of 1995, Sec. 10(e).

17   Commission of the European Communities, "Commission Opinion on Hungary's Application for Membership of the European Union", (Brussels, 15.07.97; COM (97) 2001 final).

18   Ordinance No. 118 of 1999.

19   Ordinance No. 118, Sec. 2.

20   1999, Act 263, (on the internet in English: www.uvo.gov.sk/vo_e.htm).

21   1999, Act 263, Article 2, Sec. 3. v & x.

22   Regional Environmental Center, *Doors to Democracy*, pp. 158–159, Szentendre, Hungary, 1998.

23   Act No. LXIII of 1992. For a discussion of the Act and related background information see Hungarian Civil Liberties Union, *Data Protection and Freedom of Information*, Budapest: 1997. The report is published in English and includes a translation of the Data Protection Act.

24   Article 19, Sec. 3.

25   Article 2, Sec. 3.

26   Article 19, Sec. 4. One exception to the above rules is that: "Unless an Act provides otherwise, data generated for internal use and in connection with the preparation of decisions shall not be public within thirty years following their inception." (Article LXIII of 1992, Sec. 19(5)). However, according to the legal experts interviewed, the apparent intent of this section is to protect drafts of proposed regulation prepared by a ministry, rather than to protect commercial information.

27   Act IV of 1978, Sec. 300.

28   Case No. 528/A/1996. (28 November 1996).

29   Data Protection Commissioner Recommendation Relating to the Publicity of Concession Contracts, Nov. 1998.

30   Law No. 69/1991, Article 49, sec. i.

31   For background information on freedom of information in Romania see Andreescu, Gabriel; Stefanescu, Manuela; Weber, Renate, *Access to Information in Romania,* Center for Human Rights, Bucharest: 1996.

32   Ordinance No. 118 (1999), article 44 (as modified Ordinance No. 202 (1999) published in Official Monitor of Romania, Pat I, No. 431 (31.VIII.1999).

33   Article 26 (Sec. 5).

34   Section 10(1).

35   Section 10(2).

36   1998, Law No. 228.

37   Id., Article 7.

38   For discussion see McDonagh, *Freedom of information developments in Europe,* from the *Freedom of Information Review,* pp. 58–61 Australia: August 1995.

39   70th Session, 29 April 1982.

40   Declaration, *ibid,* Sec. II(c).

41   93/730/EC Supplemented by Council Decision 93/731/EC.

42   Council Directive 90/313/EEC. For extensive analysis of access to environmental information see ed. Hallo, *Access to Environmental Information in Europe* (1996, Kluwer Law International) and Regional Environmental Center, *Doors to Democracy* (1998, Szentendre, Hungary).

43   *Federal Law Gazette* I 1997/75, (Reissue), Sec. 56.

44   *Code Administratif,* Loi no. 78–753 du 17 juillet 1978, modified by Loi no. 2000–321 (12 April 2000) (www.cada.fr).

45   *Id.*, Sec. 6.

46   Commission d'Access aux Documents Administratifs, *Guide de l'acces aux documents administratifs,* (3d. Edition 1998).

47   Commission d'acces aux documents administratifs, 9e rapport d'activite, p. 15.

48   Commission d'acces aux documents administratifs, 9e rapport d'activite, p. 13.

49   However, three German states (Brandenburg, Berlin, and Schleswig-Holstein) have adopted freedom of information laws.

50   Laws of 2000, Chapter 36.

51   Laws of 2000, Chapter 36, Sec. 43.

[52]   Open Government, *Code of Practice on Access to Government Information*, Guidance on Interpretation, Cabinet Office, 1994, Paragraph 13.3.

[53]   Freedom of Press Act, Ch.2. On the Public Nature of Official Documents. Article 2.

[54]   *Ibid*, Article 3.

[55]   Access to Information Act, Sec. 20(1).

[56]   *Air Atonabee Limited v. Minister of Transport*, 27 F.T.R. 194, 207 (1989).

[57]   5 U.S. Code Ann. Sec. 9(b)(4). For discussion of the commercial exemption under the Freedom Information Act see American Civil Liberties Union, "Exemption 4, Business Information", *Litigation under the Federal Government Open Government Laws* (Ch. 6, pp. 75–85, 1992); Kuersteiner and Herbach, "The Freedom of Information Act: An Examination of the Commercial or Financial Exemption", 16 *Santa Clara Law Review* 193–213 (1976).

[58]   Public Citizen Health Research Group v. Federal Drug Administration, 704 F.2d. 1280, 1288 (D.C. Cir. 1983).

[59]   (Report prepared with British Government Research Fellowship). (Contact address for publication, rsb@clara.net). Also see Baxter, "Public Access to Business Information Held by Government", *The Journal of Business Law*, May 1997, pp. 199–219.

[60]   1999, Law No. 118, Article 55, (Official Monitor of Romania, Part I, Nr.431/31.VIII.1999.

[61]   Act XL of 1995, Sec. 31.

[62]   Administrative Procedure Code, No. 71 (1967) as amended by No. 29 (2000). Sec. 9 (1).

[63]   Act 283 of 1993, Sec. 24 (1).

[64]   Act LXV of 1990, Sec. 14 (2).

[65]   1992 Act. 23, Section 21(5)(a).

[66]   See e.g. European Parliament, Directorate General for Research, "Measures to Prevent Corruption in EU Member States" (Legal Affairs Series, JURI 101, 03-1998) .

[67]   Recommendation No. R (2000) 10.

[68]   Acts of 2000, Ch. 22, Local Government Act of 2000.

[69]   Law No. 91–3, Art. 1 (1991) creates the committee.

[70]   The Danish Public Administration Act. Act No. 571, Part 2 (Disqualification) (19 January 2000).

[71]   The complete texts of most, if not all, U.S. state laws are available on the internet. In addition, state agencies which are responsible for enforcing conflict of interest laws commonly prepare reports which summarize their laws, which are also available on the internet.

[72]   Kennedy and Beck, "Interest of Public Officers in Contracts Prohibited by Law", *Southern California Law Review*, Vol. 28, pp. 335–347 (1955); "Conflict of Interest in Public

Contracts in California", *California Law Review*, Vol. 44, pp. 355–377 (1956); Kaufman and Widiss, "The California Conflict of Interest Laws", *Southern California Law Review*, Vol. 36, pp.186–207 (1963); "Pennsylvania's Public Official and Employee Ethics Law of 1989: Strengthening the Faith and Confidence of the People of the State in Their Government?", *Dickinson Law Review*, Vol. 94, pp. 997–1029 (1990); Davies, "Article 18 of New York's General Municipal Law: The State Conflicts of Interest Law for Municipal Officials", *Albany Law Review*, Vol. 59, pp. 1321–1351 (1996); DeSario and Freel, "Ohio Ethics Law Reforms: Tracing the Political and Legal Implications", *Akron Law Review*, Vol. 30, pp. 129–152 (1996); Lawrence, "The Proposed Michigan Government Ethics Act of 1999: Providing Guidance to Michigan Public Officials and Employees", *University of Detroit Mercy Law Review*, Vol. 76, pp. 411–482 (1999).

73   For background about transparency issues in Romania see Centre for Human Right, "Access to Information in Romania" (1996).